Love Searches
Love Responds

Preparation for Impact
a special ops search & rescue guidebook

Dr. Melonie Janet Mangum

Poetry by Melonie Janet Mangum
Scriptures in NIV unless noted.

Contents

Thank you for your insights and help:

Fran Hallgren, Jean Lubin, Gil Mertz, Vanessa & Tim Propersi, Karen Roberts, Janet Stone, and Patricialyn Taylor

Introduction

"History hinges on a single pivotal event: the sacrificial death of Jesus Christ on the cross. There, God's great redemption of mankind was accomplished - a rescue mission that culminated at the end of Christ's three-and-a-half-year public ministry but began before the world was formed," wrote Skip Heitzig in Bloodline, Tracing God's Rescue Plan from Eden to Eternity.

Jesus came with a dual purpose—to seek and to save the lost. Your heart is to do the same. You are a "special operations ambassador" of Christ. You are one of his search-and-rescue team members. You are equipped and empowered to save lives.

When an airplane fails to arrive home on schedule, thousands of dollars and hundreds of hours of labor are invested in locating exactly where it went down. The most sophisticated lifesaving equipment may be on standby, but it will be of no use unless survivors can first be found. Half the rescue is completed when the searchers locate the lost. The other half is the actual rescue operation.

Jesus clarified that the work of the Kingdom is a search-and-rescue mission. In Matthew 10:11, Jesus says, *"Whatever town or village you enter, search..."* and in Luke 15:4, *"Suppose one of you has a hundred sheep and loses one of them. Doesn't he leave the ninety-nine in the open country and go after the lost sheep until he finds it?"*

The history of evangelism is a colorful history of unlikely heroes characterized by willing hearts with a deep desire to help people rather than well-trained ability. Evangelism requires people from all experiences and backgrounds to say yes to search and rescue missions. The word means the spreading of a message of good news. Are you still wondering, "Who me?"

Don't forget when you are self-evaluating that Jesus himself was from Nazareth, a nothing village in a nowhere place (Luke 4:16, John 1:46).

Evangelism is not something we do *to* people, but *for* people, as we are led by the inspiration of the Holy Spirit. Over time, the most effective evangelists have learned how to give away the little they felt they had in the beginning. The word and work of evangelism can seem scary. What I want to communicate in these pages is a can-do spirit to encourage everyone to share the love of Jesus within their own settings and personalities.

"Think of what you were when you were called. Not many of you were wise by human standards; not many were influential; not many were of noble birth. But God chose the foolish things of the world to shame the wise; God chose the weak things of the world to shame the strong" (1 Corinthians 1:26-27).

Personal Reflections

How has the term evangelism changed over time in your thinking or experience?

Look up the scriptures below. Highlight any verses that stand out to you today.

Read John 3:16. How would you share this verse if someone asked you what it means?

Consider looking further into how Jesus evangelized. Read Mark 1:17 and the parables in Luke 10:25-37 and Luke chapter 15.

What do these parables have in common?

Search Preparation

What do you think? Are you prepared to search effectively? My husband is an FAA flight safety pilot. He says, "The flight rescue team may have its emergency transmitter locator turned on to pinpoint the lost plane. But, if they do not go searching for the signal, they will never rescue the people. You have to put legs to the signal to locate its source."

A farmer could have his harvesting tools ready, but if he remains on his front porch, there will be no harvest. Fishermen may have their fishing nets in their hands, but if they do not launch out into the water, they will not catch a single fish. You get the idea. It's not enough to think you know what to do. You must step out and begin searching.

Our mandate from Jesus is to GO—to board the search plane, walk into the harvest field, or launch out into deep waters. We must move toward the lost, confident that the Holy Spirit knows how to rescue them. You may be surprised to discover the ones crying out to be rescued are closer than you think.

Luke 5:7 (NKJV), *"So they signaled to their partners in the other boat to come and help them. And they came and filled both the boats so that they began to sink."*

Love Searches Love Responds

Reaction brings you to a conclusion. Response brings you to a process. Prominent leaders are not emotionally driven but are purpose-driven. They are great responders!

Your devotion to your Lord and Savior Jesus Christ has tremendous power. It's your heart to connect your local serving efforts to God's invincible, eternal, global purposes. I trust a renewed focus on the supremacy of God and his love for humankind will reignite passions and cultivate creative communication. It will transition any meager abilities into a transcendent anointing, flowing with the Holy Spirits' ability to initiate and sustain life. Ask the Holy Spirit to lead you.

As you pray for the pre-believers, it will engender a heart plant in good soil for God to fill you with compassion. I have often begun my week asking God to give me opportunities to share with at least 5 people about the love of Jesus, even if it's a tiny seed of thought. I have always found it a joy to keep asking for more opportunities than I thought were possible. My friend, Dona, reminded me that in my everyday shopping, school visits, and life, in one month I had the privilege of sharing God's good news of love and acceptance and praying with over 90 people to receive Jesus as their Lord and Savior. I don't remember, but I am grateful that she does so I can celebrate the Holy Spirit's leading and God's faithfulness on behalf of the seeking ones. Jesus knows the soil of their hearts. He knows who is ready for some plowing, planting a tiny seed, or harvesting a full crop of God's love.

Mark 4:20, *"But these are the ones sown on good ground, those who hear the word, accept it, and bear fruit, some thirtyfold, some sixty, and some a hundred."*

Personal Reflections

How would you describe the type of soil you were when you first heard of God's love?

Has the seed sprouted and produced more? Share a little about your journey with someone.

Consider reading Mark 4:3-8 and 14-20. What are some ways you have shown spiritual seeds?

Prayer

Father God, I believe the life-giving presence of the Holy Spirit is increasing our revelation of your eternal caring and commitment. It's not an emotional component, but a Spirit-filled igniting of LOVE'S SEARCH and LOVE'S RESPONSE. Help each of us engage! Amen! (so be it)

Revealing

Ben Williams writes in <u>Robbing Hell</u>, "Revealing has to do with bringing people into encounters that experientially show the reality of God. We get to introduce people to Jesus and not just tell them about him. It is important to note that revealing the existence of God is central to giving a true place for belief to be birthed. It is therefore about the basics of presenting the Gospel of the Kingdom."

"Responding has to do with interacting with people in a way that is meaningful and honoring to them. Responding keeps us connected to the person in front of us and not to a script or a mandate."

Jesus came to save that which was lost. What was lost? It's important to improve our understanding of the targeted group by researching their lives. As we do, we have a better chance of focusing where it will make a difference with the central message of the good news of the Kingdom of God.

"For He has rescued us from the dominion of darkness and brought us into the kingdom of the Son he loves, in whom we have redemption, the forgiveness of sins." Colossians 1:13-14.

As I am writing this section amid the corona virus quarantine, I received an email from Tyndale announcing free resources available to the body of Christ currently in stay-at-home lockdown (April 2020).

"For us here at Tyndale Bibles, a light that has shined through this darkness is the coming together of the community of believers to be innovative in sharing God's love in a time when so many desperately need it."

The Holy Spirit will reveal not only God's heart but innovative ways to respond by reaching into lives with his goodness.

Faith explores what revelation reveals. It's time to step up our search by exploring where they live, who they are, and how to be a kingdom-of-God search and rescue responder.

Kingdom of God

It's more than a what. It's a Who.
It's His presence, His power. It's You!
It's Him and His rule and reign
It's His goodness, His glory - your gain.
It's hope, The Way, and reward.
It is Jesus Christ where and when He is LORD.

Personal Reflections

What fears are still relevant to your choices?
What concerns keep you from stepping into a conversation regarding your faith or an aspect of Jesus? Are there interracial concerns? What about cultural or legal concerns?
Are there considerable financial differences that could cause hesitation?

Prayer

Holy Spirit, I seek and trust you for wisdom and direction in every decision I make. Help me and those around me find the wisdom to follow the path of your faithful promises.

My Story

"Don't ever do that again." It wasn't said sternly, but firmly. What did I do?

I had enough faith and biblical knowledge for the presentations. But I soon learned that was not all I needed. I still remember my shock the first time I preached a "good news" sermon in front of hundreds of people. The great evangelist Romeo Corpuz had turned to me afterward and firmly stated, "Don't ever do that again." What had I done?

I traveled to the Philippines leading a team to speak in evangelistic gatherings. It was not only my first time speaking before thousands of people, but it was also my first time preaching an evangelistic message in that culture.

I stood staring into the gathering of thousands of men and women, patiently waiting for the opening announcement. My heart pounded with the desire to please God and impact their lives with his love. Hearing my name reverberating through the immense speakers, I had a giant grin on my face and jubilantly bounced to the microphone. What was my message that evening? Don't have a clue. I remember being a bit surprised the interpreter flowed right along with me, with barely any hesitation. Since I was the guest speaker, the local leader gave the invitation to receive Jesus into their lives as the one who loved them so intensely he was willing to die to express the fullness of that love.

When Romeo Corpuz bellowed the passionate invitation in his native language, my chest vibrated with the power of the Holy Spirit as he spoke. I had never experienced anything like it. What was he saying? No idea, and yet the impact was unmistakable. Then in English and Tagalog, I heard him roar in a deep, God-ordained, power-impacting voice, "RUN TO JESUS!" Chairs tumbled over as the crowd rushed toward us.

13

I stood there stunned, watching people race toward the stage. Their hands were raised, and their eyes filled with determination and desperation. Healing miracles poured over the thousands at such a rapid pace we couldn't keep up with what was happening or to whom. What words can describe such a surreal experience?

I slept little that night, thinking about the glorious miracles I had just witnessed. I was desperate to learn how to have that level of impact. "Please, Romeo," I asked, "how can I improve?"

He was caring and honest as he responded, "Don't ever do that again."

My heart sank, but I mustered up the courage to receive his admonishment. I desperately wanted to improve. His answer surprised me. "It's a good thing I was your interpreter," he replied. "I knew what you were trying to say and interpreted your heart in concrete terms. I used words they could relate to through their senses, rather than abstract concepts that speak only to the intellectual understanding of a concept."

Seeing my sincere desire to learn, Romeo continued giving me examples of when I had been too abstract, assuming the audience would understand what I meant. He pointed out my use of the words fire, passion, and several other metaphorical words. "Don't just bounce the ball with these metaphors of friendship, honor, or even religion or love. Shoot for a basket with concrete truths by telling stories illustrating each concept."

In that watershed conversation, I realized the night before I had given a message without knowing the culture of the listeners. I could tell their daily lives were drastically different from my own, but I hadn't considered it in my choice of descriptive words. Trying not to look too devastated, I humbly thanked him for his advice and began my research.

When it was my turn to speak again, I wanted not only to please God, but I also desperately desired to please Romeo.

I believed his advice was constructive and prayed that my words this time would be relationally effective. Had I found concrete examples that would speak into their lives? Would they respond to the life-giving words of Jesus I had prepared? I deeply desired to fill the gap in their knowledge of God with his heart in ways that spoke clearly into their culture and lifestyle.

Did my message that evening do its intended work? Thankfully, yes. That trip was a landmark discovery. It has continued to impact the way I share the love of our heavenly Father and his Son, our personal Lord, and Savior.

If you desire, turn to the Abstract or Concrete Communication section for more clarity on the difference between speaking in concrete or abstract descriptions. Also, in my book, Glory Connections, you can read the full story.

Personal Reflections

Have you ever had a similar experience on your journey? If so, what did you learn that helped you share the good news?

Prayer

Holy Spirit, I am asking for a supernatural impartation in CQ, cultural intelligence, that will help me speak into hearts in my world.

Look and Listen

Listening is key to good communication. Discovering God's heart for a specific group of people takes a listening approach both to the Holy Spirit and research. His heart is best served when we move out of the internet researching and go among the people, listening to them about their lives. Research not only changes how we feel about them but also how we choose to interact and connect relationally as well as spiritually.

When we think about how Moses and Joshua researched the people of the land, it validates our intentional research. God told them they were to possess the land and gave them research instructions. When we think about how Jesus spoke into the culture of his day, we realize the benefits of knowing the people God is inviting us to impact. He used everyday life examples to make his point like bread, fig trees, farming, rocks, and fishing.

"Look," said Jesus, *"the fields are white unto harvest"* (John 4:35). You, on the other hand, might be thinking, "I'm looking, but I see nothing that looks like 'white unto harvest'! What am I missing? What do you mean by white fields ready to be harvested?"

Moses commissioned the spies he sent out to survey the Promised Land with these research instructions (Numbers 13:18-19): *"See what the land is like and whether the people who live there are strong or weak, few or many. What kind of land do they live in? Is it good or bad? What kind of towns do they live in? Are they fortified or not?"*

The point here is that you are to be intentional, specific, and informed in getting to know the needs and lifestyles in your targeted areas. You are to be actively searching for the lost. You must believe there are those waiting for you to arrive. Trust God's workmanship to enable connection and restoration.

The Holy Spirit is with you to redeem lives and expand the Kingdom of God.

In your search and rescue mission, sift your human logic through God's perspective. Be thoughtful not to reduce the search initiatives down to your limited understanding. Present your plans before your heavenly Father. Does your thinking agree with the concepts and ways of Jesus recorded in the Bible? As you take time to listen prayerfully, you will find your mind renewed with his generous ingenuity.

Reinhard Bonnke's post on Facebook 4.6.2020:

I heard of a theologian and a scientist being rowed across a lake.

The theologian asked the boatman "Have you any knowledge of theology?" "No!" "Then a quarter of your life's gone."

Then the scientist asked the boatman "Have you any knowledge of science?" No, he did not. "Then that's half your life gone".

The boatman said nothing and kept on rowing. After a while, he asked them both "Have you any knowledge of swimming?" No, neither of them had. "Well," said the boatman, "this boat is sinking, so all your lives have gone."

This is a parable. Our world is sinking and needs rescue. Only Jesus saves. His Gospel is the only lifeline. We are part of his rescue team.

My Lost, Then Found Son

This story describes my experience with the Holy Spirit's ingenuity while searching.

Years ago, while shopping in a small local mall, I let go of my two-year-old son's hand to explore a display of jewelry. When I looked around a minute later, Cordell was gone. In vain, I began searching the store aisles. Where could he have gone in such a short time? The store was small, my rescue team small, just Gail and me. We couldn't see him anywhere. For ten minutes we circled the store. I ran outside pleading, "Have you seen a little boy running around?" We increased the number in our small rescue team by asking the mall security for help in our search, but no one could find a little boy in a red Sesame Street shirt. My child had disappeared.

As I prayed for the Lord to deploy the angels to help us locate him, I suddenly remembered a Scripture I had read and quoted earlier from the Message Bible. Jesus, walking on the shore of Galilee, called to the disciples in their boat, "Haven't you any fish?" (John 21:4-6). "No," they answered. Then Jesus said a curious thing. "Throw your net on the right side of the boat and you will find some." They tossed their nets on the opposite side and could scarcely haul them in for all the fish.

At first, the verses seemed irrelevant to my missing boy. I had to figure out where a two-year-old child would go. Then I thought, "I need to think like a two-year-old." In other words, I should cast my net on the "other side" of the boat. I should come at the problem from a different angle of attack, with a new perspective.

All at once, it was as if the air was clear. My friend, Gail, whispered, "I found him." Where was he? He had crawled under a tall display of glassware that was several mirror shelves high.

He was hiding underneath it with his head only two inches from the bottom shelf. If he jerked his head upward, everything could come tumbling down with glass shards scattering everywhere!

My "net" was full. I had found him, but now what? Gail whispered to me again. "You get in front, bend down, and whisper his name. When you do, I will grab his legs from behind and pull him out quickly before he has a chance to react." Softly smiling and whispering his name, I bent down in his face while she grabbed his legs and swiftly pulled him toward her! The shelves were safe, he was safe, and the glassware was safe. I wasn't left paying for shattered glassware! He was safely in my arms again, giggling, with no idea of the disaster we had just avoided.

The verses in John that had helped me find my son taught me that creative solutions are "fished out" when we break away from the usual patterns of looking. The answer is often to approach our search in fresh ways.

Jesus went through life casting his nets on the other side. His ability to find original solutions to solve problems, and express truth, emerged out of the wisdom to challenge old mindsets with new, powerful illustrations. He brought a shift of vision, an openness to what could be.

We who study Christ's life can routinely forget what a radically unique person he was. He rarely fished the same waters as others. He always saw the world differently and uncovered impossible possibilities. Breaking molds of conformity, he went about doing the unexpected. You can, too.

My church, and probably yours, has ministry goals that are similar to the objectives for the material I am presenting here. What better mission could we have, than to strategically target and help people in unreached areas of their soul discover Jesus and bring faith to life?

A side thought as I was listening to the "net" today, the internet, a Rabbi was talking about the story of the fishermen casting their nets on the other side of the boat in Jesus's direction. I found it interesting when he drew an analogy between fishing nets and the internet... describing it as another completely different type of net. Consider asking Jesus if he is leading you to learn more about how to be an effective Internet evangelist.

Scripture describes Christ's followers as those fishing for men, who are ambassadors of his mercy and grace (2 Corinthians 5:20, Eph. 6:20). He invites us to follow his example. We are to be sensitive to the leading of the Holy Spirit, as we use Spirit-led words in creative ways. We seek to fulfill the great commission of making disciples by the power of the Spirit, not our limited methods. Consider asking him if he is leading you to learn more about how to be effective in Internet evangelism.

Personal Reflections

Take a few minutes to meditate on God's gracious gift of his Spirit. What experience is being highlighted in your thanksgiving?

In what ways have you seen him fulfill Proverbs 19:6? "*In their hearts, humans plan their course, but the LORD establishes their steps.*"

Prayer

Thank you, heavenly Father, for your mercy that drew me into an intimate, profound relationship with your loving ways.

Linguistic Obstacles Removed

When we have received his eternal rescue, we are not merely delivered from our less-than past, but thrust through a gate of favor into an eternal, lively interaction with the Creator of all life! He knows people's inmost hearts better than we can imagine. He can speak their heart language to soften their resistance. They are being rescued out of eternal calamity, yes, but more than that, they are being translated into a friendship with Jesus as their personal Lord and Savior who knows how to speak their language.

Matthew Jacoby writes in <u>Deeper Places,</u>" The message of the Bible is always in need of translation so that the force of its meaning might be felt through every linguistic obstacle that might present itself. One of the greatest obstacles between our hearts and the linguistic force of Scripture is familiarity. When words cease to have their designed effect, new words must be sought to instill timeless truth with fresh force."

I have had experiences where I knew the Holy Spirit had led me to listen intently and honor the person's worldview while discovering a Spirit-led transition to communicate effectively. Understanding the meaning of words in a particular culture or age group is valuable.

It is also vital to understand their worldview and values. Take a little time to do a dependency check. Ask yourself, "How much are you leaning on the Holy Spirit in your communicating?" We want to be informed on how to communicate successfully as much as possible, but it is paramount that we trust the Holy Spirit's leading as we speak.

I recently heard a minister say, "In certain strands of evangelicalism, we sometimes think it is necessary to humiliate someone's way of seeing life, someone who has a different worldview.

21

We think unless we destroy what they currently hold valuable, we cannot preach the gospel of Christ." After hearing that thought, I wanted to quote my mentor Ap. Naomi Dowdy from Singapore. I could just hear how she would respond, "WRONG THINKING!" When you are trying to reach hearts, please be sensitive to what they hold valuable. See objections and questions not as something to be rebuffed, but as a cry of the heart. People are more than some logical problems waiting to be solved; they need the person of Jesus Christ.

The strategy in this guidebook is to share successful verbal bridges and practical researching ideas that help you take the next steps for maximum impact in your targeted area. This will help you bring transformation that develops into effective impartation and activation in evangelism.

You are empowered to do this. He will not leave you without the enablement needed to be on his team. Expect the unexpected. Be willing. Try something different. Trust the Creator of the Universe.

Progressive Inspiration

Jesus led his followers by what might be called "progressive inspiration or progressive revelation" of who he was and how to live in the Kingdom of God. I first heard this teaching from Apostle Naomi Dowdy from Trinity Christian Centre in Singapore. She helped me appreciate progressive transitions in seasons and cultures. The Greek philosopher Heraclitus said, "the only thing constant is change." We can all relate in our world today and at times the changes have been so drastic and swift, we are stunned.

Jesus was their living transition to Father God, giving them access to the creative voice, message, and expression of his inexhaustible love. He summoned them to follow his example, radiating life, and by extension, he is also summoning us to seek our best creative selves to accomplish his mission.

Progressively Becoming

In Philippians chapter three, Apostle Paul describes the magnificence of his growth in knowing Christ Jesus as his Lord. He fervently declares his awareness of the priceless privilege (the overwhelming preciousness, the surpassing worth, and supreme advantage) of knowing Jesus and of progressively becoming more deeply and intimately acquainted with him. He is not saying he was already living out perfection in his spiritual and moral resurrection life in its fullness. But he was pressing on to lay hold of it by forgetting what was behind and straining forward to what was to come.

"Never be afraid to trust an unknown future to a known God," Corrie ten Boom.

God's creative love is calling out to us to become progressively more like Jesus, but it's not just in character. We are becoming seekers of truth, artists of life, creators of new possibilities, and innovative problem solvers. By looking at Jesus' life, we can observe the creative Spirit at work. This understanding inspires us to invite the Holy Spirit to awaken our creative possibilities.

Some people see Jesus as only a teacher. They think of teachers as givers of information, and they think of learners as seekers. Jesus was both a seeker and a teacher. He went to where the people were, and he taught them there.

The religious teachers of Jesus' day expected learners to only come to them and be in synagogues. Jesus not only went into synagogues and temples but also went out to where the people lived (Matthew 4:23-24, 9:35, 11:1, Mark 1:14, etc.).

23

- He went to Samaria to talk to the woman at the well.
- He journeyed to the Gadarenes, rescuing two men who were possessed by demons in Matthew 8:28.
- We read of many other places recorded in the New Testament. He was always found doing what they had never seen done before.

Most people evaluate their current lives and potential future based on what has worked well in the past. What's the old saying? If it's not broken, don't fix it. Jesus tells those following him to cast their nets in another direction. He looks inward, upward, and forward for direction, design, and destiny to be revealed.

Personal Reflections

Consider reading Philippians chapter 3. In what ways can you relate to Paul?

How has your view of God changed during different seasons of your life?

How has your altered view affected your daily life?

Prayer

Thank you, Jesus, for not leaving me stuck in old patterns of thinking that were irrelevant or just not as effective as they could have been. Thank you for bringing the newness of life into my understanding.

Jesus The Storyteller

Jesus didn't outline a systematic theology or doctrinal statements for them to follow when he commissioned them to GO. Instead, his example was to be enough with a few simple instructions. Through the years, they heard him tell timeless stories. He told a story about a mixed-up boy who ran away from home and a bridegroom late for his wedding. He told a search-and-rescue story about a woman searching her house for a lost coin, and a shepherd searching for his lost sheep. By using the vivid language of images and metaphors, he made the profound truth simple, easy for them to understand.

Transformation is God's creative expression of life. It takes place through progressive inspiration. Noah heard the voice of God sharing his will for humanity through progressive inspiration or one-step-at-a-time revelation of a new direction and understanding. God told him he was going to judge the evil on the earth in a new way, through a new thing called a flood (Genesis 9:17). Noah believed in God, even though he could not yet envision the upcoming transformation. He followed God's direction for implementing a rescue mission.

God gave Abraham different directions, with purposes unbeknown to him at the time. Abraham acted on the progressive inspiration he was given. He had choices. We do too. What if Abraham had been resistant to any of those directives, including the one regarding offering his son to God?

God's provision for the need differed from what Abraham thought it would be. He provided a ram caught in a bush (Genesis 22:13). In this incident, God revealed his ways are not our ways. God wanted Abraham's heart, not his son. Face it. We don't think like he does without his help.

God is speaking to his children today to give us a variety of practical directions for this upcoming era of the church, his kingdom on earth. The Holy Spirit may have already given you an inkling, but you know it is wisdom to wait for more understanding to unfold. Or, as yet, you do not know but are open and ready to hear how he will direct you. Faith is settling your soul as you trust his timing. You will know all you need to know as you step into his progressive inspiration.

Consider how God transformed Elisha after the passing of Elijah (2 Kings 2:15). His peers acknowledged the transformation. They saw a greater anointing with unique displays of God's purpose and plan through the legacy of Elijah, now being fulfilled in innovative ways through Elisha.

The choice of Esther as queen would have been a great surprise to anyone who knew her. God positioned her for his purposes. She was commissioned to save her nation from destruction. God's progressive inspiration and strategy for change came to her through her relative Mordecai (Esther 2:20).

Who are we now? What season are we in? What strategic changes (Matthew 9:17) are coming for the new expansion of the kingdom of God on the earth? Is it your determination to be filled with the design, direction, and empowerment of the Holy Spirit?

In the New Testament, Jesus said he would give his followers the keys to the Kingdom (Matthew 16:19). What is a kingdom? It's where his sovereignty leads and rules. Father God has confirmed and blessed not only his words but his ways throughout the ages with his presence and backing. He does not change, but his progressive inspiration, opening up creative strategies, does change with each setting, season, and era.

Even though his creative love is revealed in new ways, it never changes from the solid foundation in Christ Jesus. It begins in us when we are willing to have our thinking renewed.

We gain a richer Kingdom mindset and Kingdom vision as we process life with his perspectives for our present and future.

Have you noticed our world reinventing itself at least every three to five years? Lately, it seems the transformation is yearly. We must adjust to these changes within the foundational truths of the written Word of God, the Bible. We must lean into listening to the Holy Spirit. We are expecting his guidance to show us how to confront and embrace change while we seek first the Kingdom of God and his righteousness (Matthew 6:33). We must listen to his promptings and leadership. Then, our creative ideas and expressions will evolve to meet the needs of the times.

He is ready to inspire us with new strategies. The Bible wisely states that new wine can't be stored in an old wineskin because it will burst, and the wineskin will be ruined in Matthew 9:17. We cannot live as old wineskins, trying to fit the new wine into our old formulas. Instead, we are to learn how to manage change in creative ways.

Your team is ready to receive God's outpouring of the new wine of the Spirit into each of you, his new wineskins. You are being prepared to let it flow into robust activities, empowered to rescue, renew, and recharge.

Think about when you first accepted Jesus and the new perspectives that kept changing your mindset as you grew in understanding him. I am sure you would say yes if I asked, "Do you now understand God, salvation, holiness, the character of Christ, and the power of his Holy Spirit more than when you first prayed a prayer of repentance?" This change in you is an example of progressive inspiration. It leads you to transformative, strategic actions to complete the search and rescue mission into the area he has commissioned you to impact.

Surprise

Where there is creativity, there is a surprise. Jesus majored in the unexpected, doing things that took people's breath away and went straight to their hearts. When Lazarus died, his sister complained that if Jesus had been there, Lazarus wouldn't be dead. Jesus shocked her by calling her brother back to life, turning the funeral into a surprise party filled with the glory of God (John 11:38-44).

Winds often speak of change in literature and Scripture, as in the term "the winds of change." The 2020 and 2021 coronavirus outbreaks have radically changed our world. History testifies that those who grasp the impact of change are those who are effective in navigating the future. Let's pray and purpose to be that kind of history maker. The Holy Spirit, who fully grasps the impact of change, is within us to generate understanding and wisdom as we process how to respond to our current winds of change. His inspiration in us results in practical innovations—a new day, a new way. Rather than becoming conformed to the ways of the world that do not align with God's ingenious approaches, we are being transformed into a fresh likeness of his glory.

We can be redesigned to impact the world with the love and purpose of Jesus Christ, the Son of God. We will be informed and amazed by his movement in the body of Christ. It may seem like only a small ray of hope in the near future, but God has a plan to uncover, resist, recover and restore what the enemy has stolen. Jesus is LORD!

Personal Reflections

I'm sure you are leaning in to catch the Holy Spirit's vision for leading people into eternal life in your area. What now? That's the question of our hearts because of the difficult and drastic changes in our world today. Only he knows.

Prayer

Father, Son, and Holy Spirit, I am asking, seeking, and knocking until your vision forms as my own.

Vision

Catch the vision?
Isn't that like trying to catch the wind?
That would be true if the natural eye
was all you could see through.

You don't see the wind that turns the windmill,
yet round and round it goes.
You can't see the God that commissions you,
yet by faith, His love unfolds.
The breath of the Almighty brings inspiration.
His plan for your life is beyond anyone's imagination.

Ask your heavenly Father to instill His manifested pleasure -
his Divine will.
Ask for the desire that hope brings.
Receive your vision from the Creator of all things.
Look up to heaven. Take a deep breath; take time to hear.
Cup the hands of your heart and catch the wind.
Continue to move in his grace, following Him.

Job 32:8

Team Discussions Regarding Change

Think about the changes in church life around the world because of the 2020 pandemic. Did it affect your Christian worldview and everyday life? Following the initial lockdowns came racial violence, destruction, and devastation. The question going forward is, "How will all these drastic changes continue to transform your ministry?"

One of the global churches posted on Facebook a list of facts for the future for their leaders to consider in their action plan. I have included a few of their thoughts for your brainstorming times.

Ask your team if any of these recommendations below should be considered and how they would alter how you design events. If you are planning for an event or ministry that is not considered a mainline church as Aglow International, put the name of the ministry in place of the word church.

Think about the current online ministry options. Could it be that the online ministry is for the unchurched and basically for the non-Christian? If so, it would reach people who don't go to church or your ministry setting. The online could be an introduction to Christianity and thereafter to you and the ministry you represent. If that is true, the online presence of your ministry would be more of an appetizer for people to check what you offer. It is a lower commitment, less intimidating half step. What then would be needed to consider when developing the online programs?

- They must have a roadmap leading (almost nudging) the interested seekers toward the on-site relational opportunities in your ministry.
- The online in this case would not be considered as a substitute for already on-site times together.

- The online could also be for those who cannot physically get to an onsite gathering because of distance, travel, or sickness, etc. Therefore, there may be a need for a deeper discipleship program development.

Ask

Talk with your team about what makes people want to come to an in-person on-site gathering. What is non-downloadable? What part of your time on site will they NOT be able to get online? How could you facilitate closing this gap?

Possibly answers like fellowship, corporate atmosphere, face-to-face ministry, Holy Spirit encounters, serving, purpose, belonging, warmth, vibes, and energy, discipleship, real-life, real-time, on-the-job serving could be valid.

What else will your onsite times offer? Look for other questions that bring clarity.

Personal Reflections

A good question is powerful. As a master of change, Jesus brought people into surprising encounters with God by asking questions rather than making statements. *"What are you looking for?"* (John 1:38). *"Do you want to get well?"* (John 5:6). *"Do you love me?"* (John 21:15). *"Why do you not understand what I say?"* (John 8:43). His creative approaches drew people into unexpected transformations.

Have you been asked a simple question that changed your thinking?

What are the unexpected transformations that changed your perspectives?

Amazed

Have you heard the real estate tip that says that the value of a home is often determined by its location?

The Jews assumed the Messiah would ride into Jerusalem on a white charger, but Jesus pulled in on a donkey (Matthew 21:5) with children and palm branches celebrating his entry. Instead of ushering in his Kingdom with a sword, he chose the cross as you search your printed or digital bible for the word amazed. How many times did Jesus amaze people with the who and the where he brought life? Jesus related to people in a way that broke the tradition and opened doors to unimaginable encounters.

The Jews of Jesus's time expected the Messiah to break the tyrannical government's back. To their surprise, Jesus admonished them not to break it, but to lighten it instead. It must have been a shock when he explained what he meant by telling them if they were forced by a Roman to carry his gear a mile, go two. (Matthew 5:41).

Zacchaeus was a wealthy, thieving tax collector who was curious about Jesus. He must have heard Jesus was nearby. He was a very short man who couldn't see over the crowd gathering around Jesus. Determined, he climbed up in a sycamore tree to see him since Jesus was coming his way. "When Jesus reached the spot, He looked up and said to him, 'Zacchaeus, come down immediately. I must stay at your house today. "So, he came down at once and welcomed Him gladly." (Luke 19:5-6)

If you and I had been there, we might have been critical of Jesus for associating with someone like Zacchaeus. We would have been even more amazed to see Jesus at home dining with the man's friends and family.

Jesus' caring ways, including his surprise request to go home with Zacchaeus, brought radical mindset changes. Jesus rescued and transformed that thieving tax collector's life while enjoying his company in his home.

Jesus often picked the most unlikely person or place, and by mirroring to them what they could be, he spoke it into being. His disciples once found him sitting by a well talking with a woman from Samaria, which was taboo at that time (John 4:27). Exclusion from "sinners" was the religious rule of the day, but Jesus "tossed his net" toward unconditional acceptance.

Radical Reversals

The Savior consistently displayed an uncanny interest in the poor, sick, imprisoned, demonized, and despised. He touched lepers, got friendly with a demoniac, and pronounced forgiveness on the ones who drove nails into his hands and feet to hang him on a cross. His ways were radical reversals from all forms of prejudice.

Jesus taught his disciples God's ways were higher than their ways, by redefining relationships when he wrapped a towel around his waist at what would be their last meal together. He washed their feet as a servant would do for a master (John 13:5). The gesture of humility was too much for Peter, as it might be for us. Jesus was intentionally setting a ground-breaking new precedent of unity and acceptance. The Messiah scrubbing feet was Jesus at his creative best in that time and place of history. He rocked the conventional ideas and put everyone on equal footing in a communion of mutual sharing, serving, and solidarity.

As we read the stories of Jesus throughout the New Testament, we discover how his creative and unconventional ways were both welcomed and impactful.

His goal was to "seek and save the lost" (Luke 19:10). He did so in innovative and sometimes shocking ways.

Jesus' life punctuated radical reversals in their understanding of God as their heavenly Father and what it meant to have a relationship with him. He faced opposition and conflict as he showed the practical application of these new mindsets. Most creative people can relate. Their actions challenge people to rethink what they believe are the best ways to get things accomplished.

In Jesus's case, it was the religious elite who gave him the hardest time. They were exasperated by his claims and his violation of their rules and traditions. Yet Jesus loved the Jewish leaders so extravagantly that he refused to ignore them. Instead, he confronted them head-on. And time after time, he was unpredictable in how he went about doing it. Occasionally, Jesus captured the Pharisee's attention by comparing them to snakes, hypocrites, and blind guides (Matthew 23:13,16 & 33). Other times he responded to them calmly with his questions or gave answers that threw their current mindsets off balance (Matthew 23:33).

His indignation was obvious when he observed the poor being exploited by money changers in the Temple. He threw over the tables enlightening the money changers regarding the purpose of the Temple. It was supposed to be a house of prayer, not a place for thieves (Mark 11:15-19). Was his action to show compassion for the poor, passion for holiness, or both? Did he always respond to wrongful actions in the same manner? On another occasion, rather than show his strength, he refused to resist being arrested and passively handed himself over to his accusers. In both cases, it was unexpected.

Jesus blasted expectations of what it means to seek and save, rescue and redeem. In every aspect of his life, from his unlikely birth in an animal stall to his dazzling emergence from a garden tomb, he dared to be his radical self.

When he informed the disciples that his ways could be emulated by those following him, it must have been mind-boggling. He even predicted his disciples would do greater works than he had done (John 14:12). He modeled what could be true as they followed his leading.

It often seems easier for us to envision our lives through the lens of what we think we can accomplish. It feels more comfortable and seems reasonable to remain settled in our current life and ministry patterns. Therein lies the dilemma.

The cross of Jesus amplified and exemplified the acts and ways of God. It fulfilled the law. It changed how people can receive his supernatural newness of life. It showed a radical departure from old ways of thinking and acting into something referred to as resurrection life.

Casting one's net on the other side feels like risky behavior. At times, it is truly a radical reversal. The thought of breaking out of our commonplace ways to search for and help people surrender to the leading of God's will, as has been pointed out, is a leap of faith. But it is the only way to open ourselves to the creative abundance God desires to unleash through us. (Micah 6:8, 1 Peter 1:2, 2 Peter 1:2, Jude 1:2)

Personal Reflections

- What needs to be recalibrated for impact in your current practices?
- What could be brushed away as no longer usable in your era and season?
- What do you keep for another day before any decisions are completed?
- What might he be leading you into that you have never considered?
- What was totally out of your paradigm, your worldview, that you are now willing to investigate?

Prayer

Almighty God, the source of our life, we acknowledge you as the creator. We are one human family and endowed with great dignity. Help us see each other as you see us. Help us realize we were created in your divine image. Grant us your grace in eliminating the blight of prejudice from our hearts, our communities, our social and civil institutions.

You loved us into being and are sustaining us with your care. Keep watch over our hearts so that the evil of prejudice will not find a home in our hearts. Give us strength to mourn with those who mourn and to weep with those who weep. Let your justice roll like waves on the shore. Let your righteousness and love flow from us like rivers of living water. Purify our hearts and fill us with a genuine hunger for justice, mercy, and true peace (Micah 6:8). Direct our spirits to work toward Kingdom justice and Kingdom peace.

In Jesus's name, in thankfulness for the price he paid on the cross for our sins, we come boldly before the throne room of grace to receive the help we desperately need. Fill our hearts with love for you and our neighbor so that we may be reconciliation ambassadors in the Kingdom of God. Through our Lord Jesus Christ, your Son, who lives and reigns with you in the unity of the Holy Spirit, one God, forever and ever, I pray.

Genesis 1:26-31 – God created humanity in His image
1 Corinthians 12:4-11 – Believers are the Body of Christ,
Luke 10:25-37
1 John 3:11-18 – Love must not be mere words
1 John 4:7-21 – Those who say they love God must love their neighbor
John 15:1-8 – The Vine and the Branches
John 15:9-17 – Love one another
John 17:11-23 – That all may be one

You have prayed and now it's time to purpose once again to listen to the leading of the Holy Spirit as you move into action.

Discover the Heartbeat

Again, plans are important. But, more importantly, is listening to God's heart and the heart of the people who live in your targeted area. My most repeated plea before The Father is my request to become an intimate, one-flesh heartbeat of his presence on behalf of those around me.

How can you discover the heartbeat of your targeted area? John Dawson, in Taking Our Cities for God, wrote, "Ask yourself the question, 'Why is this city here? 'Is it merely a product of geography and commerce, or does God have a redemptive purpose in mind for it?"

Listening to both the people and your heavenly Father can be simultaneous. The process is often referred to as 'missional listening. During Jesus' days on earth, massive needs were pressing around him (Luke 8:43). If you haven't yet, you will come to a similar realization. Jesus took time to withdraw from all the challenges and desperate pain of those he was sent to rescue. He knew it was necessary to go to a solitary place to spend time with and listen to his Father.

The discovery process can be overwhelming without interaction from your Father in heaven via the Holy Spirit's voice of wisdom. The Holy Spirit will both encourage and direct you. When my teams are getting ready to step into a setting with desperate needs, I remind them that mercy without faith can be tormenting. What would faith-filled compassion brewing in a hot pot of wisdom look like today? Only in Christ Jesus our Lord, equipped by the Holy Spirit, we can remain healthy and focused as we face the vastness of the rescue mission. Keep in mind it is God's search and rescue mission. You get the privilege of being on his team.

"Faith is trusting in advance what will only make sense in reverse," Philip Yancey.

Faith

Faith makes the outlook calm
The uplook constant
The inlook accurate
Faith makes yesterday a stepping stone,
Today a limitless possibility,
And tomorrow, an endless joy!

Ask yourself, and your team, how they feel about your targeted area. Be honest. Expect a wide variety of responses. If you lived in Jonah's day, you might have been shocked at his answer to that question. God assigned Jonah his targeted area, the city of Nineveh, and his plan for reaching it. Jonah knew God was merciful, but he didn't want the Ninevites to experience his mercy. In Jonah's way of thinking, they didn't deserve mercy. He was surprised at God's heart for them. Jonah had an inkling about mercy, but he didn't love mercy (Micah 6:8). He wanted the people of Nineveh to be castigated. He wasn't even faintly interested in rescuing their relationship with God.

Personal Reflections

Read the full story in the book of Jonah, chapter 3. How did he react to God's directive toward Nineveh?

Why do you think he responded the way he did?

Prayer

Help me, Holy Spirit, to respond to life's conundrums led by your character and not just my own.

Love Mercy

In 2 Kings, chapter 7, we read a marvelous story of what it means to love mercy. There was a great famine in Samaria. People were starving, and death was at the door with no hope of being rescued. The prophet Elisha speaks into the situation and promises food by tomorrow. It was an impossible thought for those who heard it.

There were four leprous men at the entrance of the gate; and they said to one another, "Why do we sit here until we die? If we say we will enter the city, then we will die from the famine. If we sit here, we die as well. Now therefore come, let us go over to the camp of the Arameans. If they spare us, we shall live; and if they kill us, we shall but die." What have we got to lose?

They got up before full sunlight and went to the enemy's camp and, to their amazement, it was empty. The Lord had caused the Aramean army to hear a large army of chariots, so vast it caused them to desert the camp. When these lepers came to the outside area of the camp, they realized no one was there. They began to shuffle as fast as they could to the food still warm in the pots. They rushed from tent to tent, scavenging for new clothes, silver, and gold. As fast as their impaired bodies could move, they found places to hide their newfound bounty.

Can you imagine their excitement? What must they have felt, discovering everything they needed, lying there waiting for them? Incredible! Shocking!

It didn't take long before they started to ponder this extravagant provision. Something inside convicted them what they were doing wasn't right. "This day is a day of good news, but we are keeping silent; if we wait until morning light, punishment will overtake us. Now therefore come, let us go and tell the king's household."

They were unwelcome lepers who had suffered rejection every day. Yet, now they had become more concerned about the great need of the starving walled-in people than themselves. Anyone would understand if they justified themselves by thinking, "I don't care about them, that's their problem. When did they ever show mercy to us?" But instead, compassion rose inside. They realized they not only had good news, but news that could save lives.

They came back to the city and told the gatekeepers, "We came to the camp and behold there was no one there, nor the voice of a man, only the horses and donkeys tied, and the tents just as they were."

At first, no one believed them. But the king relented and sent scouts to validate their story. To their astonishment, they found everything was just as the lepers had reported, clothes, equipment, food, and as Elisha had prophesied.

What are your paramount concerns today?

They were compelled by compassion to go as fast as they could to tell the starving people what they discovered. They had tremendous, life-giving, transforming news. It wasn't for next year. It was for right now.

Who would have guessed they had the potential of bringing life into a life-threatening, impossible situation?

Who would have guessed rejected, diseased lepers would find a God-answer and become his ambassadors to save a city?

Who wouldn't be rattled by the recent news headlines we read daily about death, hatred, racism, poverty, and desperation? When you ponder this story of the lepers saying to one another, "We are not doing right," what are you thinking? You have good news too. Ask yourself, "Are you going to remain silent?"

Do you sometimes feel like leaders are the blind leading the blind?

Isaiah 42:16, *"I will lead the blind by ways they have not known, along unfamiliar paths I will guide them; I will turn the darkness into light before them and make the rough places smooth. These are the things I will do; I will not forsake them."*

Submit your concerns to him. It's imperative during these times to actively choose to do as 1 Peter 5:6-7 challenges.

"Humble yourselves, therefore, under God's mighty hand, that he may lift you in due time. Cast all your anxiety on him because he cares for you. Be self-controlled and alert. Your enemy the devil prowls around like a roaring lion looking for someone to devour. Resist him, standing firm in the faith, because you know that your brothers throughout the world are undergoing the same sufferings." (AMP)

It's not about feeling guilty, nor is it about doing your religious duty. It is about The Compassionate One, Jesus Christ, radiating his caring Spirit into your soul. His Spirit can inspire you, compel you, to recalibrate, reach out, risk, and rescue. He will lead the way.

They were overwhelmed with the abundant provision! What an adventure they had! They were transformed by the good news and their transformation became the transformation of a city as they shared their discovery.

We Are Here!

In the New Testament, we marvel at the mercy Paul and Silas expressed toward their jailer. They had been brutally beaten, bloody, and chained in stocks. God performed a miracle by sending an earthquake so severe the chains fell off and the prison doors flew open. They could have escaped as free men.

The jailer knew if the prisoners escaped, he would be castigated. He was ready to kill himself rather than face what was coming. Before he committed suicide, Paul and Silas shouted from the dark cave, "We're here!" They cared about his life more than their own in that supernatural moment. Mercy triumphed over pain.

Personal Reflections

Think about the stories. Why would the lepers consider keeping their discovery a secret? As you consider this question, think about your world today. Are there racial upheavals, economic crisis, confusion or pandemic lockdowns, trauma, and tragedy around each corner of life? If so, how would that affect your response when you think about keeping what you know a secret from those who might have mistreated you or could reject you now if you go to them?

Do you relate to any of their concerns?

Consider reading James 4:17.

Mercy's New Territory

Pioneers, heart responders, are risk-takers, trail blazers, and ground breakers. They discover what others have never seen or understood. No matter their title or workforce, they lead the way into new territory. Your targeted area is God's territory. The people there are made in his image (Genesis 1:26). He has a plan in his heart for your area, and when he looks at it, he sees the individual faces and has mercy for each one.

I believe you desire to love mercy. You have experienced transformation, and you want to tell others about it too!
The Holy Spirit is increasing your bold faith. Say yes to supernatural life. You are getting ready for an adventure. You're not going to put it off for another time. You have decided to make a difference, show compassion, and reach out.

CUTTING EDGE

Mercy is the cutting edge of purity.
Triumph is the galloping horse of faith
that leaves judgment as the slain in the street.

MERCY'S LEAD

Mercy is the impetus to zeal.
Compassion is the forerunner
of the purging, equipping,
fiery consummation of His justice.
Mercy is the catalyst that thrusts you forward
capturing the kingdom of God fervently,
for oneself and others.

REMEMBER MERCY

Law's fulfillment in Christ desires your faithfulness
to remember mercy on behalf of justice's
indictment of grace that sets the sinner free.
Sacrificial acts of reasoning's appeasement
are of no avail for mercy's wise ways
to capture souls for Christ.
"My cup runneth over."

Prayer

Taken from <u>Prayers that avail much</u> by Germaine Copeland.

Father, in Jesus' name, I thank You that the love of God has been poured forth into my heart by the Holy Spirit Who has been given to me. I keep and treasure Your Word. The love of and for You, Father, has been perfected and completed in me; and perfect love casts out all fear.

I am Your child, and I commit to walk in the God kind of love. I endure long, being patient, and kind. I am never envious and never boil over with jealousy. I am not boastful or vainglorious, and I do not display myself haughtily. I am not rude and unmannerly, and I do not act unbecomingly. I do not insist on my own rights or my own ways, for I am not self-seeking, touchy, fretful, or resentful. I take no account of an evil done to me and pay no attention to a suffered wrong. I do not rejoice at injustice and unrighteousness, but I rejoice when right and truth prevail. I bear up under anything and everything that comes. I am ever ready to believe the best of others. My hopes are fadeless under all circumstances. I endure everything without weakening because the love of God in me never fails.

Scripture References: Romans 5:5, 1 John 2:5, 1 John 4:18, 1 Corinthians 13:4-8 AMP, Romans 12:14 AMP, Matthew 5:44, Philippians 1:9-11, John 13:34, 1 Corinthians 3:6, Daniel 1:9 AMP, Ephesians 3:17 AMP, Romans 8:31, 39

Where Do We Begin?

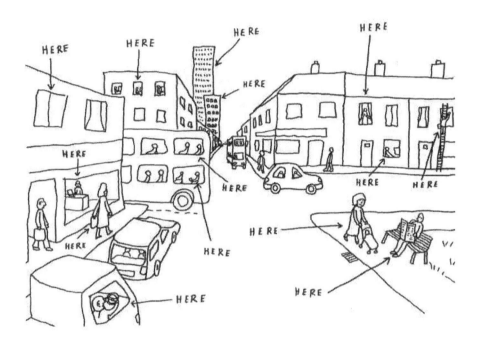

Discovery Process Speed Bumps

Before you offer a regular meeting, Bible study, trauma healing training, or outreach to your community, neighborhood, village, city, or area, this guidebook is suggesting you take the time to talk with your team about your discoveries regarding:

- What their lives are like?
- What time do they have available?
- What their struggles are?

Suppose you went out to eat in your targeted area and your waitress walked up to your table with a huge platter of noodles. She sat it down in front of you, and said, "I didn't go to the trouble to take your order because you looked like you were hungry for noodles, so here they are!"

You would be startled and even annoyed. After all, if she was truly interested in serving you, wouldn't it have been better if she had done a little personal investigating first by asking you what you wanted to order?

In the same way, taking the time to work through a discovery process will show the people that you care enough to see and identify their desires and genuine needs.

You now realize that while individuals and families are alike the world over, they differ widely based on cultural worldviews. Your searching unveils discoveries that go beyond facts. You have uncovered some necessary speed bumps in your research. You slow down to take the time to show genuine caring. It requires reaching into the heart of their world in ways that say, "I truly care about you and the people of this area, and someone bigger than me (us) (God) does too."

You've considered what God is accomplishing by prayer, listening, and researching.

You've looked for what the devil might be initiating. You've analyzed needs and discerned whether it is best to slow down regarding serving in a particular outreach right now. You may need more time for extended prayer and research before you begin. When you believe you have discovered where you or your team can make a Spirit-led difference, it's time to develop a strategy for drawing people in your targeted area to Jesus. You will soon be ready for a practical action plan.

Once your research is finished, it will enable you to be more acquainted with their personal lives. You will have a stronger base for understanding how to bring the message of Jesus into their active reality. Then you won't be guessing or just hoping. You will be effective in communicating with Jesus in both their good times and their struggles. You'll see more clearly how you can come alongside to bring what Jesus offers — "life and life more abundant" (Romans 5:17). You will discover his open doors for bringing his message into their reality.

Discovery Steps

Ask

What do I see that reveals the devil's work in my targeted area?

What do I see that reveals God's work in the area?

Where do I see a gap, a need, or an unfulfilled desire?

Who are the people of peace in the area?

What resources has God given?

How can we join what the Holy Spirit is already doing?

Below are essential steps to discover God's heart for a targeted area.

Analyze Gaps
Devise and implement a gap analysis discovery process to get better acquainted with your targeted area's needs and desires.

Apply Prayerful Listening
Ask for God's insight as you target specific streets or communities with strategic prayer approaches. You could walk or drive them as you pray (observation tours).

Share Insights
What did you see, hear, or feel from the prayer times? What did you discover from the research or interviews?

Develop an Action Plan
Brainstorm with the research findings from the personal interviews and internet research to develop a search and rescue plan.

Act
Decide on what and when you will do each step in your plan. Consider how you will handle any potential challenges you believe could happen. Assign team members their roles in the action plan.

Gap Analysis Interview, Interrelate and Interconnect

One of your research tasks is to discover the major gaps in the community's life. Here are a few simple questions related to the spiritual life of the area. For an excellent list of key questions to ask when researching your city's history, see Taking Our Cities for God, page 85, by John Dawson. Also, Discovering Your City, Bringing Light to the Task of Community Transformation, by Bob Waymire & Carl Townsend, is loaded with a variety of surveys and helpful information. It includes guidelines for interviewing and urban analysis.

- What churches or religious organizations are present?
- What are their programs?
- Do they have active outreaches?
- Do they have strategic partners in their outreaches?
- What new believer training do they offer?
- What major cultures are represented in your area?
- Are cultic or occult groups present or targeting your area?
- How large is the influence of each religious presence in your targeted area?

Another part of your research is discovering what the social needs are in the area. Here are some questions to answer.

- What desperations are obvious?
- What is the suicide rate compared to other areas?
- Is there an active human trafficking problem?
- How about abuse or drug addiction?
- Do young moms and dads both work outside the home, or do a majority have one stay-at-home parent?
- What is the economic condition?
- How does the economic condition affect how people interact with each other in their community or outside of it?

- Do any residents live behind tall walls or in gated areas, shelters, or on the streets?
- What are the felt economic needs in your area?
- How has (or did) the corona virus affect them?
- What are the most recent natural disasters in the area? (earthquakes, floods, tornadoes)
- What social services are available to the residents?
- What else do you see that is pertinent to the discovery puzzle the Holy Spirit is putting together with you?

You will need a notebook or electronic device for the research note-taking. Of course, don't forget your spiritual magnifying glass for discovering the hidden things the Holy Spirit is ready and willing to reveal.

Gap Analysis Survey

Date _____

Your Name

_____

Area, city, state, community

_____

POPULATION

Avg Family Size	Outstanding Age Groups (if any)	Ethnic groups	Demographic trend

ECONOMY

Income (upper/ middle/l ower)	% of unemployed	% of working women	Single moms raising families	Recent changes in the economy

If any recent changes in the economy, why? (disaster, factory gone, etc.):

_____

INDUSTRY / BUSINESS

Factories / Large companies / Small businesses	Farming / Recreation (tourism)

Local industries supporting the area (if any):

_____

RESIDENTIAL DISTRIBUTION

Inner city / Urban / Suburban / Rural	Private homes / Rental properties / Condos / Apartments	Homeless	Distinct ethnic or racial clusters

MINISTRIES

How many	New or old	Denomi national or not	Full Gospel / Women's or Men's programs	% of the population attending church	Attend in self-help groups

Other ministries represented (e.g., YWAM):

_____

Location:

_____

Focusing on what needs:

_____

EDUCATION

Elementary through high school	Pre-schools	Vacation schools	Business schools	Local universities & colleges

<u>OTHER CATEGORIES</u>

Active clubs & social groups:
_____

Adolescent pregnancies & abortions:
_____

Area/community programs for free or lower-income pricing:
_____

Inadequate or substandard housing:
_____

Inadequate services to elderly / handicapped / single females:
_____

Substance abuse and programs offered:
_____

Crime and juvenile delinquency:
_____

Teen and adult suicide:
_____

Racial tensions:
_____

Social challenges:
_____

High-risk danger zones:
_____

Volunteer opportunities:
_____

Gap Analysis Short Sample

Here are the results of a completed gap analysis as an example of the background information you might obtain:

- About 2/3 of the women work outside the home, largely in factories.
- The average family is low-middle income with three to four children.
- The founders were Swedish immigrants in the early 1900s.
- Many of the residents are of Scandinavian descent.
- There are eight churches. Two describe themselves as Full Gospel in doctrine, and only one has an established women's ministry. None have men's ministries. One has a youth group event that meets weekly.
- Of the women interviewed, 70 percent said their biggest areas of concern are finances and having time with their husbands and children.

Once you have gathered your area's information, you will discover a new sense of "connectedness" with your area.

- You will be able to pray with more insight.
- You will have a better grasp of the real lives of the people.
- You will have seen and heard some of the needs firsthand.
- You will be better prepared to plan a strategy to reach the area with Jesus.

New questions like the following will arise:

- Is there any chance of meeting at the business site at a lunch hour?
- Would it make a difference if they were invited into homes in small groups offering lunch or dinner without charge?
- What life-related topics would draw people to a gathering?
- How can my ministry group fit into people's lives and provide healing or inspiration for them?
- Are people open to us coming to their home or setting more than attending a gathering right now?
- Can we spend an hour talking about a life topic on a biblical basis? (At first, it's best to keep the time to no more than one hour, if possible.)

Personal Interview Survey

Provide the one being interviewed with a copy of a ministry brochure if you have one and a brief verbal explanation of who you are representing. Possibly you could add where your local meetings are held. If your interview is on the phone or internet, you can offer to send them a copy or website information they could access while you are speaking to them.

State your purpose upfront. For example, "I'm going to be asking you five key questions about the needs in your area. I'm defining the word area as _____." Name either the specific neighborhood city, county, village, etc., so the one being interviewed understands your focus.

Ask these key questions (Let them see you write down their answers if you are in person):

From the perspective of your role, what do you feel are the three most pressing needs of _____ (adult women, teens, etc.) in the community?

What, if anything, is being done to address those needs? What else do you think could be done? Can you suggest ways that my group might contribute to meeting these needs?

Do you know of any studies or surveys that have been conducted on the needs of the area that we can incorporate into our research?

What optimistic/pessimistic trends or changes do you see taking place in the community?

After all interviews, within 24 hours if possible, it is best to send a warm brief thank you note in some form whether it's a written note sent in snail mail or an email, text or other means for expressing your appreciation.

Opinions and Attitudes

People in a position of leadership will have a wealth of observations to offer. They have strong opinions and attitudes in their sphere of influence. Make a list of people to interview. Local school principals will offer comments about school environments besides the number of children of different ages. Consider interviewing the mayor, city representatives, (village) captains or area representatives of denominations or school principals, justice of peace officers, the sheriff and other police officers, editors of a local newspaper, board of education members, government representatives, city council members, or the heads of social agencies.

Don't neglect to interview the owner or manager or baristas in a local coffee shop, a real estate company, and long-time residents on particular streets or in senior living housing are also excellent resources. Anyone who is in contact with the public or who has experienced your targeted area grow and change can offer some surprising insights.

Interview Pointers for the Process

Make an appointment, if possible, either in person, by text, or by phone. Tell those you wish to interview something about who you are and the organization you represent. Inform them you are doing a community gap analysis.

Most people will be pleased by your desire to "interview" them and will eagerly respond to the simple words, "I need your help. It will take less than 15 (5 preferred) minutes. Could I ask you a few questions?" You might have to add that you are not selling anything! If they agree, make sure you stay within your stated time frame. If they do not agree, be gracious and thank them, anyway.

As an interview begins, offer a simple verbal explanation of you or the organization you represent. Do not describe your organization with words a pre-believer might not understand at this point in their life. For example, for the Aglow International ministry, you could say, "It is a non-profit Christian organization. We've been active for over 50 years, and we're now serving in more than 170 nations. Our local group meets _____ (monthly, weekly, biweekly, etc.)" Provide a copy of the ministry mission statement IF it is a good idea for this juncture in the interview. Sometimes it is wiser to hold off until the end of the interview.

Give a simple agenda with your key questions. Doing so makes it clear from the outset that you don't have a hidden agenda or an unmentioned cause you're promoting like attempting to solicit funds.

Listen attentively to whatever is shared. People appreciate being heard.

The day after the interview, use whatever means is appropriate to thank them for the interview, such as a text, email, note, postcard, or official stationery to send a brief warm message of appreciation.

Background Facts – Observation Tours

An observation tour is an action or process of observing something or someone carefully to gain information based on what can be seen, heard, or noticed.

Collecting background facts puts you in step with biblical heroes who did so as well. Joshua took a fact-finding team into the Promised Land and "never gave up" (Joshua chapter 1). Before beginning his rebuilding project, Nehemiah thoroughly surveyed the walls of need in Jerusalem. Jesus sent his disciples out ahead of him in Mark 11.

Tips for observation tours

Notice. Drive or walk through the area. Notice billboards, shops, businesses, homes, and people on the streets. Try to see things you've never noticed before. Get a feel for the flavor of the area.

Read. Find out what local newspapers, magazines, signs, and internet sites say regarding the area.

Connect. Check out the Chamber of Commerce, City Hall, health services, and other social agencies and government offices. What have they posted on their offices, walls or websites, etc.?

Survey. Do a telephone, internet poll, or written survey to sample opinions of people in your area. Be friendly, polite, ask permission, and keep questions simple. You can use forms, printed and/or electronic, as tools for collecting the basic information you need. You can then add other questions.

Action Plans

Any enterprise that is built by wise planning becomes strong through common sense, and profits wonderfully by keeping on top of the facts. (Proverbs 24:3-4).

A tiny car beeps its horn and rounds a corner. As it does, a sticker becomes visible that reads: "When I grow up, I want to be a large heavy truck." Now that's a car with a big dream!

What are your dreams for God's life-giving ministry of love and purpose in your targeted area? What direction have you chosen to get there? How will you know when you arrive?

What Is an Action Plan?

An action plan, in military language, is a battle strategy. You've been rallied to war by our great Commander-in-Chief Jesus to release captives from darkness and death into a quality life filled with God's blessing (Luke 4:18). Forming an action plan means spreading out your map and developing a definitive strategy for carrying out God's vision for your targeted area. An action plan lays out the details for where you are, where you want to be, and with God's grace, how you intend to get there.

Is it presumptuous to make plans like that? No. God is a smart planner. Luke 1:15 says God planned our divine purpose (Jeremiah 29:11, Romans 9:11). Plans are purposeful preparation with a willingness to be flexible whenever and wherever recalibration is necessary.

All believers are under direct orders from Jesus to display his resurrection power to defeat the rule of Satan by drawing people into his love, purpose, and leading. We have been given this commission in the name of Jesus. It's good to have a plan!

An action plan includes a specified goal for its accomplishment.

It may feel a little strange to declare it at first, but think along these lines as you are developing your plan: "I'd like to see twenty individuals or more saved this year" rather than "I'd like as many people saved as possible, as the Lord leads."

Keep in mind that an action plan is made of elastic, not concrete, meaning it's flexible. A goal of "twenty individuals or more this year" expresses concrete intent while giving the Lord plenty of room to work and surprise you. Maybe you will find, as the months go on, that while some are being saved, others are returning to their faith after years of doubt, and others are being filled for the first time with his Spirit. Also, circumstances can shift quickly, causing a need for your plan to be recalibrated, bending with the moment. A natural disaster, for example, can cause a shift in your strategy. A good action plan does not freeze; it flexes. Finally, keep in mind that an action plan is a toolbox, not a test of your leadership.

How Can an Action Plan Benefits You?

Maybe you're thinking, "This kind of planning takes too much time. Let's get out there and minister!" If so, I strongly encourage you to consider these benefits of a well-formed plan.

- Helps you express God's vision and keep it in the front of your mind
- Stirs others to action
- Rallies others to follow
- Focuses on your time, talent, energy, and money on what matters most
- Helps you grow in responsibility and accountability

How Can You Develop Your Action Plan?

Here are some suggestions to get you started.

Prepare
Set aside a special time for you, and those you are working with, to devote toward developing a plan without trying to squeeze in other business. Allow yourself as much planning time as you need. It will be valuable time spent together for the days ahead.

Pray
Set aside time to talk with God about it. You don't want to do this alone. God is ready to guide you. Be open to hearing from him in all ways—from a vision, prophecy, special word, impressions, and thoughts about facts you have gathered. Pay close attention to a Scripture that comes to mind, or a desire newly planted in your heart.

The Bible is full of wisdom for planners. Here are a few:

- Abide in Him and ask in John 15:7.
- Expect Him to instruct and teach you in Psalms 32:8.
- In Proverbs 16:3, you are exhorted to commit your works to him.
- Jeremiah 29:11 declares He is ready to give you a future and hope.
- 2 Chronicles 2:18 shows a history of God giving plans of all that the Spirit put in the minds of men to accomplish.
- Psalms 20:4 notes that He cares about your heart's desire.
- Proverbs 11:14 directs you to go to good counselors in the endeavors.
- Proverbs 15:22 and 16:1 reminds you not to listen to scoffers, but to the Holy Spirit for the best answers. Why? Because humans have plans of the heart, but from the Lord comes the proper answer of the tongue.
- Ephesians 5:15-17 brings the Holy Spirit's direction for character as you submit to one another in the fear of the Lord.

Dream

Don't get hung up on thinking you have to be certain you can achieve a goal before you set it. If a goal seems reasonable and easily achievable, you're probably aiming too low. Make it a faith goal, a God-given dream, beyond what you can reasonably achieve. Dare to risk. Less risky goals are usually sterile of God's empowerment. Faith goals require an investment of heart, emotion, time, and personal resources to make them come alive.

Connect

Your action plan should support the vision, values, and goals of those on board with you working together to reach the targeted area. Spend time with your co-laborers, sharing the discovery content as God reveals it to the group. Listen to each person's input, whether it seems negative or positive. Find common ground of heart for practical application.

Make sure everyone knows they have been heard. Let them know whether their input is going to be acted on, needs revision, or will be left for another day. People can accept disagreements or different plans when they know their ideas and feelings have been validated. It's when they feel ignored they become frustrated.

Assess

Take the time to assess/evaluate your plan. Does it adequately address the needs? Do the chosen actions align with the stated goals? How do you see the Holy Spirit leading you to meet the needs and your stated goals?

My church decided to offer quarters and soap once a week at the local laundry service area with no agenda, just relationship building. Now people are asking them questions about why, who, where, etc., because they took the time to meet a need.

More questions to consider asking your team.

- While asking the questions, listen to responses that give you a clue if you are in unity of function, purpose, and heart.
- What are the strengths and weaknesses of your goals?
- When you identify weaknesses, which ones need to be redesigned or strengthened? What would you need to do so? What does your team NOT want to take with you into this next season?
- What will you need in resources—workers, time, energy, and money—to help your plan be successful?
- What about the skills and spiritual gifts of the people you are working alongside for this plan? How will your plan engage them?

The following are a few of the many online surveys to help you and your team identify spiritual gifts.

heart2heart.org - Don and Katie Fortune's motivational gifts
gifts.churchgrowth.org - Spiritual Gift Survey
lifeway.com - Spiritual Gifts Assessment Tools

In a 2020 post, Mario Murillo posted the following thoughts:

"The gifts and anointing of the Holy Spirit always come through relationship. Sorry, but Christianity has always been, and always will be, family-owned and operated. So then how can we know our assignment? God will give you a way that is unique to you. The secret of finding your assignment is in your heart. God speaks to the heart and then the heart must control the mind."

After taking one or more of these surveys, ask yourself and your team how their heart and abilities could be incorporated.

Ask which activities are for the team at large, and which activities should be an individual assignment?

For example, is there someone on your team that enjoys research? How about someone who enjoys doing interviews? I have a good friend, Fran, who enjoys doing budgets. She says it's fun, like putting together a puzzle. I need Fran on my team. The makeup of your team's personalities and skills will determine which activity suits them best. You will also be able to discern which activities are better accomplished individually or as a group project.

Besides personal resources, you also must assess financial resources. What are the finances needed to accomplish your plan? As much as is possible, try not to let your current financial resources limit the Holy Spirit-led and faith-filled plan. Instead, keep your eyes on what you believe God is leading you to do. Building the resources for each endeavor usually has its own approaches, whether it's the sale of items, fundraising from good-hearted givers, or _____. Brainstorm with your team potential avenues of financial resource for your events.

Commit
Having set your action plan, commit, begin, and stick to it until it's time to re-evaluate. Don't file it away in an unused, dusty corner of your mind. Keep a copy of your action plan around where you can re-read and reference it regularly. Find ways to remind each other on your team. If you talk about it, you will more readily walk it.

Re-evaluate
Depending on the magnitude of the plan, re-evaluating every three months is a good idea. Don't let any old, ineffective goals keep you tied to what is not productive. Familiar approaches may feel as comfortable as a pair of old shoes, but don't keep using them without considering what the Holy Spirit might initiate for an upcoming change – comfortable or not. The plan that seemed so good in January may need some adjustment by June.

<u>Celebrate</u>!
When part of your plan succeeds, stop, and rejoice! It's easy to get caught up in the labor pains of ministry and not notice the sweet work of God when it's only a small blessing along the way to the greater goal. Before you rush breathlessly on to the next task, stop. Go out for a treat together, send each other notes of congratulations, or buy each other a single flower or another small victory gift.

Action Plan Ideas

Target large or key areas where there is little effective Christian influence. The Holy Spirit rarely asks believers to isolate themselves in a particular home, restaurant, or building, but asks them to go out and about in the mainstream of life.

In other words, whenever advisable, go where the people are. Consider being a part of community gatherings such as fairs, parades, and festivals. You might be able to set up a booth or table at a gathering to draw people to you. If you can, offer an attractively designed handout. An encouraging Psalm with various Scriptures from the book of Psalms is a surprising way to engage people in conversation. Or, if you have equipped people, you can offer dream interpretations. Of course, some of these can be offered via internet video apps like goggle or zoom. Books like Steve Sjogren's <u>101 Ways To Reach Your Community</u> are helpful for ideas.

Don't forget the power of offers to pray. At one community event in a local park, a team put up a sign that read "What's Prayed Here Stays Here." People came requesting prayer.

Attending Chamber of Commerce meetings can be a good way to learn about and volunteer in city events. It also helps you get to know the people who have a heart for the community. When the time comes, you can ask to present your idea for an event. When you do, consider bringing a gift for the meeting such as a basket of edible goodies.

Conversations

"Let your speech at all times be gracious (pleasant and winsome), seasoned (as it were) with salt, (so that you may never be at a loss) to know how you ought to answer anyone (who puts a question to you)," Colossians 4:6 (AMP).

Colossians gives us good instruction about our speech. In a world filled with hurt and heartache, it's never been more important to show empathy and compassion. If we want to see healing and restoration, then empathy and compassion have to involve action. And one way we can put compassion into action is by creating a safe space for meaningful discussions.

Do you always think before you speak? If not, you may experience trouble you could avoid. Very often we are not sensitive to other people. We might give correction when a person needs edification, or we may tell them something that causes them to worry when they have many other difficult situations to handle. Not only do we need to use wisdom with our words, but timing is very important. We may need to discuss a matter with someone, but if we do it at the wrong time, we will only create more problems. Ask God to give you the wisdom to know when to speak, to whom to speak, and what to say.

The Words You Use in Conversation from Your Ministry of Conversation by Randy Fujishin:

"Whether you've been a follower of Jesus for most of your life or you recently asked him into your heart, the fact that you're a Christian should be reflected in the way you speak to others in your daily conversations. Your changed heart should be clear in your changed speech.

It is the words we choose to use in our everyday conversations that will determine if we enlarge or diminish those we interact with. Craft your words with grace. It is the words we choose that will determine if we heal or hurt, encourage or discourage, soothe or anger, bless or curse those we talk to every day. In the end, it will be words that bring life or death to others.

Isn't it possible we could be wrong in our judgments because we don't know the full story behind someone's actions? My friend was often misunderstood as not caring or friendly when the reality was, she couldn't afford new hearing aids and she simply couldn't hear the conversation.

Be kind and courteous in dealing with people, for everyone is likely fighting their own hard battle. Be thoughtful. Not everything is about you. Before you assume, there is this thing called asking. Don't forget to include it in your times together rather than jumping to a false conclusion that could cause more harm. Be humble enough to ask with a desire to learn and understand. You've heard the saying, there are two sides to a story."

When you engage an individual in conversation in your search and rescue mission, first ask about the person. For example, if it's a lovely day at a park, you could open the conversation with a question about how they are enjoying the day. Then listen to their reply with a sincere desire to get to know them.

No one likes to feel like they are being baited. Check your motives. Make sure you are not connecting with them for the only purpose of gaining information, but genuinely caring about who they are. Based on what you learn by listening, when it fits naturally in the conversation, look for opportunities to share your relationship with Jesus in heartfelt ways.

Possibly, you can share how the Holy Spirit has impacted your personal experience or in your gatherings with other believers. When the time is right, invite them to join you in a gathering.

The gathering can be the two of you or a setting you feel is a good next step for their progressive understanding of Jesus.

Keep in mind that people are more likely to attend gatherings when invited in person by someone they trust. Even in our high-tech age, word-of-mouth "advertising" is always good.

Of course, don't neglect to share your pre-planned gathering information via email, Facebook, Twitter, Instagram, and other social networking sites if they are effective in the culture of your targeted area. Social networking tools enable communicating both a caring heart and information for upcoming social events.

I repeat a theme you have read in this material over and over again. In every encounter or opportunity, so many questions are answered when you first ask God to open your eyes so you can "perceive" their lives. He will let you in on innovative and effective ideas as you proceed through the processes written herein. This guidebook is a tool introducing you to some beginning inspiration, information, and practical strategies to implement the search and rescue process.

Personal Reflections

What conversations changed your way of thinking? Maybe your life?

Prayer

After reading this, what would your prayer be at this moment?

Good News Sends Us

We are followers of Jesus; therefore, we are on a mission – his mission. We make disciples of all ethnic groups by going, teaching, and baptizing (Matt. 28:18-20). We are sent to teach, speak, counsel, discuss, and proclaim the good news to others so that they might be baptized into God's new creation and join his mission of making all things new.

"Again, Jesus said, "Peace be with you! As the Father has sent me, I am sending you" (John 20:21).

We are called ambassadors of reconciliation and given the privilege of sharing in Jesus 'ministry of reconciling the world to himself (2 Cor. 5:17-20). Those who have been changed by the good news of Jesus share its life-changing power with others, so get your testimonies ready. See Training Exercise 3 for more help about developing simple testimonies.

We have the honor of announcing and embodying the good news by caring for the poor and rebuilding lives (Is. 61:4). Remember, the future for the people of God is an entirely new city in a new creation (Rev. 21). I read somewhere in the myriad of books and posts a metaphor I enjoy. "The church is to be a movie trailer of this grand, coming attraction, in which all things will be made new!"

This is Who We Are

We are devoted to Jesus and one another in the body of Christ, but also, we are to love our neighbors and our city. Since we have come to Christ, we are all sent on his mission. We are new and have a new purpose. We are reconciled and ushered into a vibrant and living relationship with God. We never separate our identity in Christ from our purpose in him. We live on a mission because we have received the good news.

Consider yourself a first responder who is ready to discover unexplored territories. Take initiative; keep praying and pushing outward to expand the Kingdom of God in unreached or lightly reached areas (2 Corinthians 10:16). Don't wait for people to be interested enough to reach out to you; help create the opportunity. Don't keep what you know a secret!

Pray others won't keep it a secret either! "Therefore pray the Lord of the harvest to send out laborers into His harvest" (Matthew 9:38).

"Then He said to them, 'The harvest truly is great, but the laborers are few; therefore pray the Lord of the harvest to send out laborers into His harvest" (Luke 10:2).

Personal Reflections

These thoughts were posted online from Chuck Pierce's church in Denton, Texas June 2020. As you read through them, be sensitive to the thoughts that strike your heart in an obvious expression from the Holy Spirit.

"There are thousands of people frustrated right now because they believe they have not tapped into who they are and what God has called them to do.

72

Likely, the Holy Spirit has been preparing them in the hidden place and he's about to release them into what he has been preparing. The signs, wonders, and miracles that have been prophesied for years, saying they were coming soon, are now being revealed. Some of you have never prayed and seen a literal miracle. Why not believe the body of Christ will demonstrate who he is in ways we have never seen manifested before? Our deep desire is for the world to experience Jesus through his body, the ekklesia, the Church."

"Now, Lord, look on their threats and grant to Your servants that with all boldness they may speak Your word, by stretching out Your hand to heal, and that signs and wonders may be done through the name of Your holy Servant Jesus," Acts 4:29-30 NKJV.

Prayer

Consider 15 minutes in prayer, exalting, decreeing, and proclaiming.

- Exalt the Lord as the Commander of the hosts of heaven, who are being sent in this era to carry out his Word.
- Decree a fresh outpouring of Pentecost has come into the earth, accompanied by signs, wonders, and miracles.
- Proclaim "The greatest harvest of souls the earth has ever seen is being reaped."

Acts 4:29-30 in these treacherous, yet miraculous, times, *"Now, Lord, grant to your servants that with all boldness we may speak your word. Stretch out your hand to heal and let signs and wonders may be done through the name of Your holy Servant Jesus."*

Father God, your ekklesia is rising with the Commander of the hosts, Jesus. Lord, pour your Spirit out once again on your people. Activate our spirits with your faith and power.

Let us be those who birth signs, wonders, and miracles into the earth. Even as at the first Pentecost, rock the world through a changed kingdom-minded, a kingdom-activated body of Christ. Change our worldview from your perspective.

Help us come into alignment with your will and ways. We trust you to do your part and we are believing by faith in the truth that we are your workmanship in Christ Jesus that we will do ours. We choose to pray and then expect you to extend your hand to heal and deliver. We choose to intercede and trust you will draw the lost to our Lord Jesus. Here we go! It is time! Cause the angel armies to be loosed in the earth. In your timing, we believe their sickles will swing far and wide, reaping the end-time harvest of souls. Send the new believers to assigned families in Christ to be baptized and discipled. We believe we are in the most amazing of days! Miracles, miracles, miracles in abundance you will bring to pass all around us. We will treat this harvest with humble, loving care as the great treasure it is, and rejoicing will fill our hearts as we celebrate with the angels every soul that is saved! Thank you, Jesus! Amen.

Decree

We are in the days of miracles and harvest!

Listening After Trauma

During your interviews, you may encounter someone who has been recently traumatized. Evaluate your time constraints. A drop-in interview may not be the best timing; therefore, you may consider offering an appointment to hear their story another time. If you decide to continue listening, these tips will help you interact with sincerity and heartfelt impact.

How we listen and respond to someone who has been through a life-altering trauma can make a huge difference in a future relationship. The listener needs to let the traumatized one share their story at their own pace. It may take several minutes or even times together before the whole traumatic story unfolds.

Make sure you show you are listening by looking at them, saying words or sounds of agreement, and reflecting sincerity in your body language. I learned a sober lesson when I was listening to a story with a broad smile on my face. I was intently listening, but the answer was so real to me, I was grinning. Her response was, "Do you think my situation is funny? Why are you grinning at me?" Lesson learned.

You also don't want them to feel like you are rushing their story. From time to time, repeat what you think the person has said. This will give the person a chance to correct, restate, or affirm your understanding.

Describing their experience could cause people to become very distressed. If you sense this, offer a break or help them think about something pleasant until they are again ready to continue. See the breathing exercise in this material.

Eventually, people need to bring their pain to the Lord themselves, but it may take time for them to do so. Be sensitive to the space you have been granted in their time and setting. Sometimes, less is more. Eliminate common cliches that attempt to bring solace, but rarely do like, "God is in control", or "You'll get over it soon."

Grieving

Give people room to express grief. Grieving is a normal reaction to trauma. What is grieving? Grieving is mourning the loss of something. This might be the loss of a family member or a friend. It might be the loss of a body part or the function of a part of the body. It might be the loss of property or position, time, or financial stability. Whether small or enormous, all losses affect us and make us experience some degree of grieving (Neh. 1:3-4). Trauma always involves loss, but we can experience loss without trauma, as with the slow death of an elderly parent.

Grieving is hard work, but some things can make it even more difficult. These can be things such as how the loss happened, or beliefs people have about grief.

When they are ready, encourage them to talk about how they feel. Allow them to express their anger and sadness. Listen to their pain. Do more listening than talking. Healing will come as they let the pain out. They cannot absorb teaching and sermons. Help the person feel at ease and assure confidentiality.

Use these three questions to guide your listening, especially if you are listening to people right after a disaster or you are going to them to show caring.

What happened?
How did you feel?
What was the hardest part for you?

Use these additional questions, when appropriate, to help the person realize that some good things might have been a part of the experience:

Who helped you?
Were you able to help others?
What gave you the strength to get through?
Did you see God in this situation?

Depending on the background and faith of the person you are asking, you could ask, Do you believe you were given spiritual help? Explain.

Using these preliminary practical questions as an ambassador of God's mercy, grace, and healing does not replace the healing room prayer times, therapy, advice from a professional, or pastor.

Listening without giving advice or quoting Scriptures is often very difficult for Christians who haven't experienced severe traumas. Their personal experiences, where advice, Bible reading, or prayers made a tremendous difference, making them believe it's necessary to share it right away. Often the willingness to just be there, listen and care is enough.

Your area, whether small or as large as a busy city, is surely experiencing drastic change and some of it could have been very traumatic. Maybe you've known your targeted area for several years, and yet you realize because of recent world events, you don't know the answer. Political, economic, and business changes are affecting the world over. People change (even if it's just getting older), landscapes change, and the culture changes within the larger global transitions.

Considering the effects of the coronavirus in 2020, with the mandates to stay in homes, businesses unable to serve the community, and job losses, there have been drastic changes worldwide.

Few, if any, saw it coming and therefore were unprepared. Are you aware of how your area is suffering or suffered during that time or one similar? Remember, intentional, authentic listening is key.

Heartbreaking events are happening in lives all around you. Be encouraged. God is ready to grant innovative ways that reflect his caring. Jesus, God's Son is your Lord and friend. The Holy Spirit is your comfort, guide, and empowerment. The Holy Spirit will help you hear his heartbeat and the heartbeats of those he is sending you to impact.

"The heart of him who has understanding seeks knowledge," Proverbs 15:14 (NKJV).

Personal Reflections Prayer

Empowerment and boldness prayer, taken from Prayers That Avail Much by Germaine Copeland.

Father God, as a member of Your royal race, I have been made a king and a priest unto you. I am your workmanship, created in Christ Jesus to do the works you have prepared for me to accomplish. Because I was born for such a time as this, I will make a difference in this generation and influence future generations. You bestowed upon me your creativity and ingenuity, and they are expanded through the power of the Holy Spirit, which you sent to be my Helper and my Strength.

Father, I believe I receive that boldness now in the name of Jesus. Therefore, I have the boldness to enter the Holy of Holies by the blood of Jesus. Because of my faith in Him, I dare to have the boldness (courage and confidence) of free access – an unreserved approach to you with freedom and without fear. I can draw fearlessly and confidently and boldly near to your throne of grace and receive mercy and find grace to help in good time for my every need. I am bold to pray.

I come to the throne of God with my petitions and for others who do not know how to ascend to the throne. I will be bold toward Satan, demons, evil spirits, sickness, disease, and poverty, for Jesus is the head of all rule and authority – of every angelic principality and power. Disarming those who were ranged against us, Jesus made a bold display and public example of them, triumphing over them. I am bold to declare, that Satan is a defeated foe, *"Let God arise, and his enemies be scattered."*

I take comfort and am encouraged and confidently and boldly say, "The Lord is my Helper; I will not be seized with alarm – I will not fear or dread or be terrified. What can man do to me?" I dare to proclaim the Word toward heaven, toward earth, and hell. I am bold as a lion, for I have been made the righteousness of God in Christ Jesus. I am complete in Him! Praise the name of Jesus! Amen.

Scripture References: Psalm 27:14, Acts 4:29, Ephesians 6:19, 20 AMP, Mark 11:23, 24, Hebrews 10:19 AMP, KJV, Ephesians 3:12 AMP, Hebrews 4:16 AMP, Colossians 2:10, 15 AMP, Psalm 68:1, Hebrews 13:6 AMP, Proverbs 28:1, 2 Corinthians 5:21

The next section has samples of questionnaires and training sessions you could use to begin your research. Alter them to fit your team and area. They are guidelines to inspire your thinking and help you connect with the ones you are interviewing.

Training Exercises

Exercise 1: Time Together Brainstorming

 <u>Warning</u>: This experience requires an open, non-judgmental mind and attitude. If you are harboring any of the thoughts below, please set them aside and be open to the experience:

- "I'm just feeling blank. I can't come up with anything."
- "I guess I'm not the creative type."
- "Maybe I just don't have the anointing anymore to be a leader or team member in this area."

<u>Safeguard</u>: "Catch a God-centered vision for engaging in world evangelization. Passion for God in worship precedes the offer of God in evangelism," writes John Piper in <u>Let the Nations Be Glad</u>. Worship and prayer open the door to brainstorming with the Holy Spirit. Therein lies wisdom and effective direction.

What Is Team Brainstorming?

Brainstorming is a creative process that frees you to accept any words and ideas as possibilities to consider. It is a group process that requires spontaneity without fear of judgment. Brainstorming is done verbally. Ideas are recorded as they are voiced.

Sometimes all it takes is a fresh perspective to free us from a mental block in our way of doing things. Have you heard the story of the trucker who attempted to drive through a tunnel with a load that was a few inches too high? He became impossibly wedged in, or so everyone thought. Try as he might, he couldn't move forward or backward. Many experts were called in at substantial cost to debate all possible solutions, including the radical idea that a portion of the tunnel is removed.

Finally, a little boy standing by the side of the road tugged on the driver's sleeve and piped up, "Mister, how about just taking the air out of the tires?" His pint-sized perspective saved the day.

You may ask, "Is brainstorming the same as the idea exchanging? I think we've already tried this." Brainstorming and idea exchanging are usually worlds apart. Idea exchanging is trading proven ideas that have worked before, sort of like an idea recycling process. But in brainstorming, the key is new ideas. Another way to say it is that it's time to exchange an "if only" with a "why not."

Brainstorming requires granting freedom for yourself and for others to let go and let the ideas fly, no matter how crazy they seem. None are to be judged as right or wrong during the process. The more untested and unheard of they are, the better! Smile, don't be afraid and dream out loud.

 **Brainstorming Guidelines**

Stage One – Blast off!

a. Relax and prepare to have fun playing with ideas.

b. Be open to each other and to the Lord. Expect the Lord to be working among you. Make sure you invite the Holy Spirit. It is reasonable to believe he will be pleased and enjoy the creative process with you.

c. Choose a leader and a recorder for the experience.

When your leader announces the goal, for example, "We're going to take ten minutes to brainstorm ways we can encourage visitors to our group to come back again."
Everyone thinks, "What if ...?" or "Why not try to ...?"

a. Everyone takes sixty to ninety seconds to silently jot down a few ideas in five or so words each.

b. When the leader and recorder indicate it is time to begin, everyone then begins speaking out ideas at random. (This may feel strange at first until you get rolling with it.) Any idea at all, no matter how crazy, is heard and recorded.

c. No one is permitted to evaluate anything said in any way, verbally or nonverbally. For example, no one is allowed to say, "But that won't work because..." or worse yet, laugh at someone's contribution. Also, everyone must take care not to make negative or positive nonverbal cues. No one should be applauded or offended for sharing an idea. There are no bad ideas.

d. The recorder posts all the ideas shared on a whiteboard, large poster board, computer screen, zoom app whiteboard, or other display devices so that everyone can see.

e. Everyone continues calling out their ideas. The goal is the number of ideas, not quality. Ideas that might seem unworkable should be shared as well.

f. When one idea shared triggers another with a minor variation, it can be shared.

g. Everyone keeps their ideas rolling until the leader indicates the time is up.

Stage Two – Landing

a. Everyone reviews the list together, with the leader acting as moderator. Similar ideas can be combined, and those agreed upon as outrageously unworkable ones can be crossed out. Decide which ideas are possible "keepers" without being overly conservative – some suggestions that might work can serve as a beginning platform.

b. Refine the keepers, remembering that an idea that seems improbable at first can develop into something that will work. (This step takes time and thought, so you can spend time doing it immediately or schedule a time to do it later.)

c. Select a few keepers and think through some ways you might put the usable ideas into practice.

Exercise 2: Mapping Out God's Land

 The area you have targeted is your land. It is also God's land. A map is only a lifeless technical drawing, but it represents individual souls who desperately need Jesus. Display your map on an overhead or printed where everyone can see it.

Begin by everyone writing on their device or paper, "Our purpose in doing a gap analysis is to _____."

Take two or three minutes to write your answer. Then share answers. Do you agree on the "why" behind what you plan to do? Without agreement on the why, there is little potential for it happening.

Look at the mapped-out area. Pray and ask the Lord Jesus to help you go there with him in the Spirit, like Joshua, to "spy out" and explore your land. Ask him to make important things obvious and to let unimportant things fade away. And praise him in advance for all he is going to reveal to you about your land and those you want to reach.

Pray specifically for street names, addresses, or other means of covering the area you have targeted with prayer.

Take notes on what comes to mind while praying and listening.

Exercise 3: Strongholds Defeated

 This experience requires you to have already researched your targeted area.

Have someone report their findings from a history check developed by previous researchers and spiritual mapping enthusiasts. Spiritual mapping is a process based on the belief that the demonic realm has territorial spirits ruling over geographical areas. John Dawson writes in his book, Taking Our Cities for God, "The earliest days in a city's history are very important because one of Satan's main strategies is to interfere with the process of birth."

Once these strategies have been uncovered, prayers and activities displaying the opposite spirit can be planned. This exercise isn't about doing that research. It is informing your team of what was uncovered by the researchers who have looked at the history of the land spiritually and pointed out certain background tactics of the evil spirits for prayer and activities for you to consider in your planning.

Take five minutes or so together to review what has been discovered about the history of your area.

- Name of area, city, village, or other.
- History of God's people in the area, especially if they have had revivals.
- History of other spiritual influences in the area positive or negative.

- Go to prayer together, asking God to reveal the "strong man" (demonic stronghold) if it hasn't been revealed thus far (Matt. 12:28-29). Releasing Heaven on Earth by Alistair Petrie is a resource for Removing the Barriers to Effective Evangelism, Revival, and Lasting Transformation. It outlines the biblical mandates for healing the land and releasing God's blessing.
- Identify the sins of your area Bring them before God in prayer "standing in the gap" for forgiveness and restoration. Ask, seek, and knock for mercy, forgiveness, and blessing.
- Exercise upper God-given authority over evil interferences against your area. Jesus defeated the devil by his death, burial, and resurrection. Activate confidence in the name of Jesus who has defeated the works of darkness.
- Take positive action against evil by choosing to act in the opposite spirit. For example, intentionally plan to be generous where greed is prevalent, merciful where unjust judgment prevails, and loving where abuse is ongoing. As you plan a project in the opposite spirit, exercise your faith in the spiritual gifts (supernatural special abilities) you are expressing. See 1 Corinthians 12:4-11. Remain steadfast by being accountable to one another, declaring the truth that his love never fails (Lamentations 3:22; 1 Corinthians 13: 1, 8).
- Alone or with your team, praise God for as many beautiful positive attributes as you can think of regarding your targeted area.

God gave Jesus authority over heaven and earth. Based on that authority, Jesus told his disciples to make more disciples as they preached, baptized, and taught. With this same authority, Jesus still commands us to tell others the Good News and equip them as disciples for the Kingdom. Be ready with your powerful testimony. Your testimony is his story – history that changed your history.

Testimony Development Tips

Let's begin at the bare bones beginning in developing your testimonies. Choose one. Is it your salvation? Is it a time when God made provision in a supernatural way?

Now think about how to boil it down to approximately six keywords. You can do this.

How many six-word biographies are there in the Bible of people? Many scriptural heroes have already been described that way.

For example, David, of whom God said, "A man after my own heart."
(1 Sam. 13:14; Acts 13:22).
Or Paul's self-description: "Paul an apostle of Jesus Christ" (Eph. 1:1).
Paul's description of Timothy: "my true son in the faith" (1 Tim. 1:2 NIV).
Consider these words about Mary: "The virgin shall be with child"
(Matt. 1:23
Description of Jesus: "Became flesh and dwelt among us" (Jon 1:14).
John wrote, "One of His disciples whom Jesus loved (John 13:23).

What six-word description would best describe you? Would it be positive or negative? Would it be "not an easy person to love" or "A shining light for the Lord?"

I decided my first words would be clueless, curious, surprised, believed, transformed. I can easily build from them my life-changing testimony.

My friend wrote, fatherless, rejected, teaching, Father, loved, identity.

Personal Reflections

Write your six-word testimony.

It's effective to prepare your personal stories of God's intervention. Your story of how his transformative power altered your life is unique to you and a powerful witness of his love. Your life story is your curriculum for compassion. Your experience becomes your student's syllabus. Your heartaches can reap a plentiful harvest in another person's life.

Get ready to tell your personal story of how Jesus has been faithful to you. How has your story merged with the story of Jesus?

Speak Into Your World

Tell others how you have found him faithful. Tell them who you know him to be. Remember, in the history in the Bible, the recounting of the stories was always relational. God's stories were to be told in the family, around the fire, or in the gatherings. God's stories were the three-dimensional microscopes that helped them understand their unique personal history. Our entire life story is but a sentence in the grand story, his story – Jesus's story. Our sentences were never meant to say everything all by themselves. It takes all of us telling our personal stories in Christ to communicate his magnificent presence, power, and eternal, transformative love.

Lee Rushing's book, Backpack Evangelism, Lifestyle Evangelism for Believers, chapter 8, gives the following outline for salvation testimonies on page 105. Consider following a similar outline for your expanded testimony.

A brief personal introduction:

My life before Jesus Christ…
How I realized Jesus Christ as Lord and Savior…
How I believed in, trusted, and received Jesus Christ as my
Lord and Savior…
What Jesus Christ has done in my life…
What Jesus Christ is doing in my life now…

He also writes, "I would also recommend some things not to do. Don't start off saying something like. "I became a Christian when I was…" Don't use words an unbeliever may be unfamiliar with – words like sanctified, justified, rapture, prophecy, sacrament, mass, confirmation, Eucharist, baptism, ordained, saved, born-again, and others – you get the idea. Write your story in a conversational tone, and as if you were sharing it with people from different backgrounds. Practice with a friend."

Remember, your area is God's area. Reach out and help the seeking ones find their destiny in Jesus. Be full of expectation in the Holy Spirit's ability to draw the ready hearts to you. Believe the commission in Matthew 28 is for you and that he is with you! Go and make disciples!

Matthew 28:19-20
"Therefore, go and make disciples of all nations, baptizing them in the name of the Father and of the Son and the Holy Spirit, and teaching them to obey everything I have commanded you. And surely, I am with you always, to the very end of the age."

Exercise 4: Listening

Small Groups – Missional Listening Practice

Arrange yourselves in small circles in even numbers. Have everyone partner with someone next to them. Ask each of them to tell one small, but traumatic event they have experienced. Not the most traumatic event that has ever happened to them.

While one is sharing, the other person listens. Listeners, listen intently, showing you understand the story. Missional listening is the goal. Missional listening means you are paying attention without being distracted, and yet alert to the input of the Holy Spirit.

Be patient. Don't quickly jump to an answer for their pain. Use the questions suggested earlier (What happened? How did it make you feel? What was the hardest part?). After ten minutes, switch roles if that is appropriate for the setting. If not, you ask the questions and patiently, compassionately give them time to fully answer with "no word" breaks in the conversation.

In a larger group IF you are practicing this as an exercise discuss:

- How did you feel during this exercise?
- Was anything difficult?
- Did you feel heard when you were listened to?
- Why or why not?
- What did the listener do well?

Exercise 5: Breathing

During an interview, when traumatic events are shared, people with wounded hearts can be overcome by strong feelings. This breathing exercise can help them learn to take control and relax. You can find video examples on the Internet.

1. Get into a comfortable sitting position.
2. Close your eyes if you like. Think only about your breathing.
3. Slowly breathe in and out, filling your lungs and slowly releasing the air.
4. Feel yourself relaxing as oxygen is flowing in and out."
5. Think about being in a quiet place. It might be the beach, or on a hill, or by a tree. You could imagine being alone or with someone who cares. Consider thinking about Jesus telling you how much he loves you.
6. Continue to think about your breathing, flowing in and out, in and out.
7. After five minutes, open your eyes. Stretch and take one more deep breath.

Exercise 6: Imagination Practice for Sharing Jesus

Activate Your Imagination

Are you looking for cues and clues to activate your imagination and prepare for effective conversations while on your search and rescue missions? Have you ever spent time storytelling with story cubes? They look like dice with small drawings. It could be a drawing of a tree, or person, or boat, really anything at all. You roll the cubes, and whatever draw comes up, you build a story from your imagination. These practice scenes can be used similar to the story cubes.

Consider choosing one or two of the practice scenarios written here to activate your sharing prowess. You or a small group of friends could engage in these evangelistic adventures. You never know if the Holy Spirit will respond by sending you to someone very similar to the ones you are imagining.

1.   College Campus Picnic Tables

If you are sharing the heart of God on a college campus, find out if there is a Christian group on campus. Some campuses have strong Christian groups and activities. They may have started Bible studies. Look on the college bulletin boards or activity websites. When you connect with the leadership of these groups about your plans, they are usually happy for the help and will pray for your activity or come alongside.

Scene
You see students sitting at the picnic tables on the campus lawn. You notice a student sitting alone, which makes your conversation easier because you prefer one to one. You walk up and introduce yourself.
Realizing timing is everything, you approach with a smile and simple "Hello, my name is _____."

Because students may have a class in a couple of minutes or are finishing up their work assignment, ask politely, "May I ask you a couple of quick questions?"

The student responds, "Sure, what's up?"
"You are going to school trusting it will change your life for the better, right? Everyone wants their goals to be accomplished and their future to be good. I am guessing you are preparing by studying and getting ready. Since you only have a few minutes, I would like to share with you what I did to prepare myself for a healthy and vibrant future that made a drastic difference for me."

(You would have previously thought through a version of your testimony, so you would be familiar with it enough to be short and to the point.)

You can tell the person is receptive, so you continue. "Not only did I prepare for everyday life, but I also prepared for eternal life. At the time, I had no idea that my preparation was going to change drastically, not only the days ahead, but transform my whole life for the good."

Share your prepared personal testimony. Include how God's love through Jesus, transformed you inside and out. How did it give you a different outlook on life?

You could share something like: "Our choices change our lives. Our studies and activities change our lives. No one person or a college degree can change a life more than Jesus, the Son of God. I am living proof."

Offer a simple example. Make sure it includes God's love for them and Jesus rescues them by forgiving them and is now inviting them into a personal relationship.

What bridge sentence could you say here?
Time is up. How would you close your time with them? What would you offer?

Remember, connecting and sharing is not "closing a deal." It is about people coming into an awareness that the Creator of heaven and earth loves them just as they are. He longs to have them with him now and forever. It's more than rescue from past sin; it's stepping into a whole new paradigm of life only God himself could give.

2. Your Are a Giver by Nature

You have desired to share with women of a different culture. You make sure you are smiling as they pass by, but as yet, you haven't figured out a way to begin a conversation. It's natural for you to offer yourself hospitality or giving. You have been longing to meet these ladies you see in the shops near you.

On several occasions, you already have tried complementing one of them on her beautiful sari, or colorful way of dressing. Once at a sales counter, you complimented an Indian woman on her sari. She jokingly offered it to you. There were a few awkward, but pleasant, exchanges back and forth, but nothing significant came from the brief encounter. You didn't even get the chance to plant a tiny seed of friendship. You have decided next time you will be brave and make more of an effort.

Scene
There she is, a brightly colored, sari-dressed woman in front of you, entering the same store. Her bright-colored sari is silky flowing in burnt orange beauty. With an inward sigh, you remember how many times you have tried to engage in conversation without success. Just as you are thinking this, the items she is carrying tumble out of her hands onto the floor. Without thinking, you step up your pace and offer to help. There's your gift of giving showing up. As you do, she says thank you and warmly welcomes your help.

You comment, "Are you returning these?" She nods yes. You respond, "Life is full of returns.

We buy something and then it's not going to work after all, and you have to take it back and start looking again."

You only have a few minutes standing in the store with her. What more do you say? What do you offer? Today only a seed will be planted, but you are thankful for even the smallest opportunity. Can you imagine anything going further?

3. White Car at the Carwash

Nothing is on your mind except home duties and a dirty car that needs to be cleaned. As you wait at the car wash, you are glad for a reason to be relaxing quietly in the light breeze and sunny, 74-degree day.

Scene
Your car is white and very dirty. You decide to go to a professional carwash and get it cleaned inside and out instead of one of those drive-through car washes.

After you turn over your keys to the cleaning crew, you walk to the patio area to wait for it to appear once again all fresh and shiny. As you sit down, there is a grandma and child right next to you.

Enjoying the sun in your face and the light breeze, you notice that most of the cars getting washed are white like yours. It's a common dilemma for you these days. When you park in a large parking lot, you have a hard time finding your car because there are so many similar ones.

The little boy is playing in a fountain while grandma watches. You jokingly begin the conversation by saying something like, "I think more people should buy white cars because we have so few here, don't you?"

She laughs. Continuing the chat, you ask, "Is one of the white ones your car?"

She responds, "Yes, that one," and points it out to you.
"Do you have as much trouble finding your car as I do in parking lots?"
She laughs again and comments, "Many times," and tells you a funny story of her lost and found car one day after shopping.
"We live in California, so I guess a white car is popular. Do you know why?"
She responds, "Maybe less hot in summer."
"Yeah, I think so," nodding your head in agreement. "My husband always likes white cars. I just got a good deal on white. How about you? What caused you to buy white?"

What can you imagine her answer will be?

Then you continue, "White always seems to symbolize purity; maybe even symbolizing a new start, a do-over. I had a do-over recently. I had another white car and bumped the side and rear into my neighbor's car. Not fun. When everything was settled, there I was again, buying another white car. That was my do-over. Have you had some significant do-overs in your life personally? Were they hardships or adventures or a little of both?"

Where can you imagine your testimony coming into this conversation after you have listened to hers? How would you begin?

4.   Teacher and Parent Volunteer

You volunteer often to help in your child's or grandchild's classroom. The teacher is beginning to know you.

Scene
It's a special event at the school. Families are welcomed to lunch with the teachers and students. The students share their artwork, and everyone roams around the lunch area and classrooms.
You have little time, maybe five minutes, but you want to begin a conversation that could be an intro later into further conversations about the Teacher Jesus and how he and his teachings changed your life.

Could you begin by saying something like the below?
"Teachers are so extremely valuable. That's why I enjoy helping in the classroom when I can. I have had some terrific teachers in my life who changed its trajectory in significant ways. Out of all of them though, Jesus in the Bible is probably the most transforming."

(Then tell why and tell a specific story and time.)

You might want to add, if true, that you didn't use to think of him as a teacher or that his teaching would have much to do with your personal everyday life.

Do you go further? Do you have a Scripture story you can share quickly? What questions do you ask after sharing?

What responses do you think the teacher could have, both positive and negative? How would you respond if the time was up, kids were pulling at the teacher, and everyone had to leave? What could you offer later?

5.   Airport Suicide Prevention Sign

You've checked in and have some time before your flight. It's not enough time to watch a movie on your computer or read a chapter, so you take a few minutes to walk around and mindlessly stare into the open spaces, watching myriads of people passing by.

Scene
You are slowly passing a 4-by-8-foot sign in the airport. You take a few minutes to stop and read the words, Suicide Prevention Hotline, with contact numbers. You sigh and decide to sit down nearby, thinking about how much danger there must be for suicide for them to post a large sign here in the airport.

As usual, people are sitting everywhere. You turn to the person next to you, pointing to the sign. "Did you notice that sign? Have you or someone close to you ever considered suicide?"

At first, the person answers no, not that they know of, and seem disinterested in talking with you. You keep commenting. "I have. I don't think I (or someone else you choose) could have taken my life. I have known others who did, and it devastated their families. Watching the effect on them, helped convince me not to put my family and friends in that horrible confusion and pain. But during a dark time in my own life, I considered it. I wanted out of here, away from all the trouble, pain, and confusion."

Give the person a space to comment or add their own story. How would you proceed if they added nothing else? How would you proceed if they told you a sad story about a friend or relative?

After listening, share what made the difference for you (or the person you know). Remember not to jump to a snappy resolution that sounds trite. Maybe it's time to add a few questions:

- "What was the hardest part for you at the time?
- "What about now?
- "Has it changed much?

What story have you heard about God, Jesus, or the Holy Spirit that drew you to him? What did the Spirit of God do that made a difference in your feelings of desperation? Remember to be thoughtful, gentle, caring, and not preachy in your approach.

6.   Server and an Acquaintance

You are an encourager by nature. It gives you delight and energy to make people smile and uplift their day. You chatted with your acquaintance who lives nearby several times as she passed by on her walks with her dog. You have learned that she loves serving in practical ways and is a hospitable woman. Each time you happen upon each other on your morning walks, you ask her what she is up to. Invariably, she eagerly responds by telling you a story of serving food for the homeless, gathering clothes for those in need, or helping in some other community event.

Servers will often respond to the gospel (Good News of Jesus) when it is presented as practical and useful. They may be inspired to talk more with you if you ask questions like "What is a man's greatest need?" or "Have you ever considered how much Jesus focused on the importance of having a caring and helpful attitude?"

Scene

It's time for your morning walk. You have prayed that she will be out at the same time as usual. "Help me, Holy Spirit, have the right words to transition our conversation from her joy of serving to You and the good news of eternal life."

As you were turning the corner, she is walking home as well. You greet each other again with big smiles and a welcome lingering chat. She begins again to tell you what she is up to in the community.

How would you step into her community concerns or one of your own?
Do you or someone you know have a testimony of serving that changed their lives you could share?

Could you begin by saying, "When I read the stories of Jesus, I_____
_____.

Create a conversation, imagine an opportunity, and brainstorm the finish.

7.   Red Robin and Wine

You and a friend are sitting in the bar area at a Red Robin restaurant. The bar area gives you more opportunities to begin conversations.

Scene

When the waitress asks for your drink order, you and your friend both order water. Instead of bringing water, she comes back again, asking what wine you ordered. She said she thought she had forgotten what label of the wine you wanted. You remind her you both ordered water.
Then in a few seconds, you add, "Did you know Jesus turned water to wine? It was his first miracle recorded in the Bible."

She responds, "Is that in the Bible?"
"Yes," you answer. You tell her the story about the wedding feast. Jesus turned water into wine at the wedding because the hosts ran out of wine. It was the best wine they had ever tasted.

The waitress seems curious about more of the story. She may have enough time to chat, or she may have to go at that moment.
If she has time to chat, consider what to say next. You could ask, "Why do you think Jesus would do such a thing?" Or you could give your testimony of how God changed the natural into the supernatural in your life. It could be a time of peace, hope, or faith.

Then decide how the conversation could progress. Imagine a unique ending to this creative encounter.
(In this true scenario, the waitress had little time, so they chatted only a little longer. Later, my friends came back to the Red Robin restaurant. They brought the waitress a New Testament marked with the story of Jesus when he turned water to wine. Since then, the three of them have enjoyed many conversations.)

8. Luncheon Healing

You have been through a particularly difficult season. Cancer was diagnosed. Praise God, you are living and responding well. Your relationship with Jesus gave you desperately needed peace during this hard time.

Scene
It's a luncheon banquet in a restaurant. A wide variety of food choices are available. People you don't know join you at your table.

As the food is being served, the lady sitting next to you seems to be staring at your plate in a nosey way. She asks, "Did you get some chicken?"
You respond, "No", but you realize she must be paying close attention to what is on your plate for some reason.
Then she asks, "Are you a vegetarian?"
"No. I lean toward a plant-based way of eating."
She is more curious now. "How did you get started on this way of eating?"

She doesn't know you were diagnosed with cancer two years ago. You had choices to go through radiation and chemo. You also felt led by the Holy Spirit to change your eating habits. Share your story.
What can you imagine she might ask now? How would you continue the conversation?

Do you share any fears in the beginning? Do you share any thought processing or faith-building exercises that helped you live in peace?

Don't become preachy, nor make it seem like it was no more than a simple formula you followed on your way to recovery.

You notice the table is listening to you. How would you transition to something about your faith? What testimony would be a good transition? Should it be a whole testimony or only a few facts?

What might their questions be, and how would you respond?

What overall thought would you like to leave for those listening, even if they never face what you faced? What wisdom is heartfelt and caring to share?

9.   Christmas Time With a Giver

There's no doubt about it, your best friend's husband is a giver. He delights in giving. People who have the supernatural gift of giving rarely desire their giving to be broadcasted. Consider questions like, "What do you believe would be the greatest gift someone could give to God?"

Scene

You are chatting in the living room, seated around the Christmas tree. You are next to your friend's husband. After the usual surface talk, you join the conversation by asking, "_____?"

No matter what you imagine his answer to the question, how would you respond? Would you ask another question?
Would you share something personal? Or would you express interest in knowing what it meant when you were given a special gift?

Do you have a personal story about a gift you received? You might want to mention that you rarely tell people about it because it is too personal.

Imagine a response. Think of something Jesus said or a parable he told that your friend would appreciate as a giver. Consider telling a brief story out of Luke 21:2.
In that story, Jesus admired the faith of a poor widow who put in her two small copper coins. You could share the complete story in a natural storytelling manner. Make sure it fits his culture and lifestyle. Remember, gifted givers will be interested when the gospel (Good News of Jesus) makes sense in everyday practical life.

10.   Frozen (movie #1)

You have experienced the Holy Spirit giving you the gift of wisdom and mercy. You find delight in translating signs, movie emphases, or book themes into messages about spiritual life in Christ.

Scene
You only have a few minutes next to the lady at the park. Both of you have children on the play equipment. You smile, say hi, and ask about her children. Do your children like the Disney movie Frozen?

Carefully and sincerely listen to her answers. If she doesn't add a reason, you might continue with something like:

"I have seen that movie innumerable times. My children (or grandchildren or neighbor children) love it. What is it about that movie?"

"This week I watched the first one with them again. As I did, I realized the very real-life drama being depicted.

(Consider a comment in the sharing about the line, "Removing ice from the heart takes true love.")

Around the world, there is an epidemic of hopelessness. Most of Disney's movies are filled with hope, but life doesn't always end in that kind of good news. Have you ever felt like your heart was turned to ice?
Listen with compassion and sincerity. A good number of people can relate. It was such a hit to both children and adults. Tell your story of a time when Jesus thawed your icy heart with the fullness of his love. How did he uplift your hope?

Below are a few concepts in the first "Frozen" movie to consider. Pick the ones that fit the sense you have while sharing with this woman:

- Fear is your enemy
- Isolation/rejection/misunderstanding
- Loneliness, hiding, but looking for love
- Love is an open door
- Don't let anyone in
- Sister Anna's love and hope never give up; faith, hope, and love press her on
- Anna pleads with her sister to come out of hidden places, delivered of fear

11.   Mary Poppins

You loved the original "Mary Poppins" movie and couldn't wait to go see the remake. You have decided to invite the grandkids. You want them to experience the delight of watching Mary descend into the sad lives of two children.

It's a holiday, and the theatre offers an inexpensive showing at 10 a.m. Why not take a friend for each child too? Your neighbor has a couple of children the same age as yours, so you invite them along.

As you are driving to the theater, you tell the children about how much you loved the movie when you were young. You share your favorite parts of the story and how they made you feel happy.

Scene
You arrive at the theater, shepherding the children in a bundle of merry chatter. You buy the popcorn and drinks, settle into the dark theater, waiting for your favorite person to float from the sky on the screen. When she does, you excitedly exclaim, "There she is! It's Mary Poppins! See how she came down with the kite!"

The movie delights everyone. As you exit, gathering them into your van, you ask them what they enjoyed the most about the movie.

How would you create a conversation on a child's level? Draw a correlation between Mary Poppins and Jesus.

What characteristics could you draw from the picture that would agree with God's heart? What about the words to the song the balloon lady begins singing at the end, "Nowhere to Go but Up?" Which lines in the song would you share with the children, correlating them with Jesus?

Life's a balloon
That tumbles or rises
Depending on what is inside
Fill it with hope
And playful surprises

And if you don't believe
Just hang on to my sleeve
For there's nowhere to go but up
Let the past take a bow
The forever is now

Another two children start nodding off in quiet tiredness as you approach home again. As they climb out of the car, their mom greets them. "Do you have time to come in and chat awhile? Thank you for taking them. Did they behave to you?"

Now it's your turn to talk to the mom as the children run off to play. Does she remember the movie? What are her favorite parts? How would you tell her how parts of the movie remind you of the stories of Jesus and his love, hope, or rescue?

Possible ways to approach your sharing heart to heart:

- It makes me feel _____. How about you?
- Both children and adults gain from the perspective of _____
- The only other place that makes me feel that hopeful, and even more so, is _____

What testimony do you share that fits here?
How do certain settings in the movie depict God, Jesus, and Holy Spirit? What is God offering us that the world does not?

Maybe a comment about the dirge of hopeless feelings that we hear so much about these days. Create your conversation with the mom, giving careful attention to her responses.

12. Compassionate Teen

(Empathetic, concerned, kindhearted, considerate, caring, benevolent)

Scene
He lives down the street, often on his skateboard or throwing baskets into the basketball net. When smaller children come out to play, you see him helping them make baskets, holding them up to reach the net. If one of them stumbles, he is quick to pick them up and comfort the child. Sometimes he walks them home if there is a boo-boo. When a car is coming, he gathers all the children to the side to make sure everyone is safe.

Obviously, he has a kind heart. How can you connect with this young man? Can you do hoops with him? If not, how would you get to know him in a conversation?

Considerate, empathetic people usually relate best on a feeling level. Logic isn't as effective. Try one of these questions:

- "How do you feel God wants us to treat each other?
- "I can see you have a heart much like Jesus in the Bible. He would enjoy watching how you treat people.
- "Do you feel there is any hope for the suffering people in the world either for this lifetime or the next?

What story about Jesus would you share that parallels his caring behavior?

Do you have a personal story that fits this setting? Now what?

Expanded Understanding of Concrete vs. Abstract Words Enabling Clear Communication

Abstract and concrete are classifications that indicate whether the object described has physical attributes. Abstract objects have no physical attributes, whereas concrete objects do.

Abstract words refer to intangible qualities, ideas, and concepts. These words show things we know only through our intellect, like "truth," "honor," "kindness," and "grace." Concrete words refer to tangible, qualities or characteristics, things we know through our senses.

In spiritual conversations, use concrete words we know through our senses, like pen, loud, sitting.

Avoid using only abstract words that we know through our intellect like bravery, honor, beauty, quickness. Abstract: She has beautiful eyes. Concrete: She has big, brown eyes.

Examples of abstract nouns include liberty, freedom, love, generosity, charity, and democracy, betrayal, courage, cowardice, cruelty, forgiveness, truth, fear, grief, happiness, jealously, sympathy, insanity, knowledge, wisdom, right/wrong, duty, fame, justice, liberty, friendship, greed, innocence, rules, social norm, and religion.

Notice that these nouns express ideas, concepts, or qualities that cannot be seen. We cannot see, hear, touch, taste, or smell these concepts.

Do you remember the old television series, The Beverly Hillbillies? Consider watching a few of the episodes on prime video or wherever you find them.

Some are fun examples of communicating in terms whether abstract or concrete that do not mean the same thing to those speaking as it does to those listening. You'll enjoy a hearty laugh. The program makes the same point about speaking with the listener's culture in mind to be an effective communicator.

Skit

Nora Corpuz, Romey's wife, wrote a skit with two main characters: a female evangelist speaker and her interpreter to help us communicate successfully. I have included a portion of her skit for you below.

The stage is set; the audience is seated. Speaker and interpreter step up to the microphone.

Preacher: When I preach, I will not beat around the bush.
Interpreter: When she preaches, she won't go around hitting our short trees.

Preacher: At my home church, many people are running around like chickens with their heads cut off.
Interpreter: Too many people (look at preacher) what are they doing in your church?

Preacher: Running around like chickens with their heads cut off.
Interpreter: Oh, in dis woman's country there is great persecution. They are cutting their heads off like chickens. We will pray for our sisters and brothers there.

Preacher: The preachers in town are not waiting on God, they are always jumping the gun.
Interpreter: The preachers in her town, (turning to the preacher) What are they doing now?

Preacher: Jumpin' the gun.
Interpreter: Oh, these pastors are putting a gun on the ground and jumping over it.

Preacher: Even worse, they are always shooting their mouths off!
Interpreter: No!

Preacher: Yes.
Interpreter: These preachers are always taking a gun, putting it to their mouths, and shooting their lips off.

Preacher: At home when we were getting ready to go to church it was raining cats and dogs.
Interpreter: What's it doing when you go outside?

Preacher: Raining cats and dogs
Interpreter: They stepped outside, and small animals began to fall from the sky.

Preacher: I confess that sometimes I get so angry with my husband, I chew him out.
Interpreter: She is confessing to us that she gets angry and bites her husband.

Preacher: Then you are in church and your husband is trying to smile but everyone can see you just chewed him out.
Interpreter: Everyone can see the blood is dripping down where she bit him.

Preacher: I know you understand because sometimes you just need to blow off steam.
Interpreter: She thinks we understand that we need to put our lips on a bowl of boiling water and just blow.

Preacher: It seems like someone is always there to quench the fire.
Interpreter: Thank God, someone comes and puts you out before you burn to death!

Preacher: People need to have enough guts to fast and pray.
Interpreter: What we need is people with big bellies to fast and pray.

Preacher: Isn't it good to be together?! Elbow your neighbor and say, "You are a sight for sore eyes."
Interpreter: It's good to be together so you can hit your neighbor and say, you make my eyes sore.

Preacher: If you will follow my words…
Interpreter: If you will talk like I do.

Preacher: The power of God will sweep over you.
Interpreter: God will hit you with a broom.

Preacher: The power of God will sweep over your congregation
Interpreter: God will hit your congregation with a broom.

Preacher: Then, you will spiritually walk in the promised land.
Interpreter: And you will find yourself dead and gone to heaven.

Preacher: What I have told you is the truth, and you can find it in the Bible.
Interpreter: This woman believes everything she said is in the Bible.

Preacher: I hope you can come to my country and help us as much as I have helped you.

Interpreter: My friends, I hope that one day some of you can go to her country and straighten this woman's theology out!

Preacher: God bless you and keep on truckin'.
Interpreter: God bless all the truck drivers.
Preacher: Amen.
Interpreter: Praise the Lord! Finally, she's finished!

Recommended Books

101 Ways to Reach Your Community by Steve Sjogren

Bloodline: Tracing God's Rescue Plan From Eden To Eternity by Skip Heitzig

Backpack Evangelism: Lifestyle Evangelism for Believers by Lee Rushing

Changing the World Through Kindness by Steve Sjogren

Completely Irresistible: Drawing Others to God's Extravagant Love by Shannon Ethridge

Discovering Your City, Bringing Light to the Task of Community Transformation by Bob Waymire and Carol Townsend

Evangelism by Fire by Reinhard Bonnke

Foreign to Familiar by Sarah Lanier

Glory Connections by Melonie Janet Mangum and Lana Heightley

Going Public with the Gospel by Lon Allison & Mark Anderson

Let the Nations Be Glad by John Piper

No More Christianese by Doug Addison

Power, Holiness and Evangelism by Randy Clark

Power Evangelism by John Wimber with Kevin Springer

Poverty and Justice Bible by the Bible Society

Prayers That Avail Much by Germaine Copeland

Prayer Evangelism by Ed Silvoso

Presents From On High by Lana Heightley

Releasing Heaven on Earth by Alistair Petrie

Robbing Hell by Benjamin Williams

Taking Our Cities For God by John Dawson

There Is More by Randy Clark

Upshift by Melonie Janet Mangum and Lana Heightley

Your Ministry of Conversation by Randy Fujishin

A practical evangelism internet class:
releasinglife.org

https://youtu.be/D7jTUfNyPkE

https://youtu.be/0Lu9qdX_2vo

M3International.org Leadership Journey 3 x 5 Leading Through Crisis:
heart2heart.org

Made in the USA
Columbia, SC
04 April 2023

14421414R00063